HANDS-ON GUIDE SERIES®

Hands-On Guide to

Webcasting

Focal Press Hands-On Guide Series

The Hands-On Guide series serves as the ultimate resource in streaming and digital media-based subjects for industry professionals. The books cover solutions for enterprise, media and entertainment, and educational institutions. A compendium of everything you need to know for streaming and digital media subjects, this series is known in the industry as a must-have tool of the trade.

Books in the series cover streaming media-based technologies, applications and solutions as well as how they are applied to specific industry verticals. Because these books are not part of a vendor-based press they offer objective insight into the technology weaknesses and strengths, as well as solutions to problems you face in the real-world.

Competitive books in this category have sometimes been criticized for being either technically overwhelming or too general an overview to actually impart information. The Hands-On Guide series combats these problems by ensuring both ease-of-use and specific focus on streaming and digital media-based topics broken into separate books.

Developed in collaboration with the series editor, Dan Rayburn, these books are written by authorities in their field, those who have actually been in the trenches and done the work first-hand.

All Hands-On Guide books share the following qualities:

- Easy-to-follow practical application information
- Step-by-step instructions that readers can use in real-world situations
- Unique author tips from "in-the-trenches" experience
- Compact at 250–300 pages in length

The Hands-On Guides series is the essential reference for Streaming and Digital Media professionals!

Series Editor: Dan Rayburn (www.danrayburn.com)

Executive Vice President for StreamingMedia.com, a diversified news media company with a mission to serve and educate the streaming media industry and corporations adopting Internet based audio and video technology. Recognized as the "voice for the streaming media industry" and as one of the Internet industry's foremost authorities, speakers, teachers, and writers on Streaming and Digital Media Technologies.

Titles in the series:

- *Hands-On Guide to Webcasting*
- *Hands-On Guide to Windows Media*
- *Hands-On Guide to Video Blogging & Podcasting*
- *Hands-On Guide to Flash Communication Server*

HANDS-ON GUIDE SERIES®

Hands-On Guide to

Webcasting:

Internet Event and AV Production

STEVE MACK

DAN RAYBURN

Routledge
Taylor & Francis Group

LONDON AND NEW YORK

First published 2006 by Focal Press

Published 2016 by Routledge
2 Park Square, Milton Park, Abingdon, Oxfordshire OX14 4RN
711 Third Avenue, New York, NY 10017, USA

First issued in hardback 2016

Routledge is an imprint of the Taylor & Francis Group, an informa business

Library of Congress Cataloging-in-Publication Data
Mack, Steve.
  Hands-on guide to webcasting : Internet event and AV production / Steve
Mack.
      p. cm. -- (The Focal hands-on guide series)
  Includes index.
  ISBN 0-240-80754-5 (pbk. : alk. paper) 1. Webcasting. 2. Video
recordings--Production and direction. I. Title: Guide to webcasting. II.
Title. III. Series.
  TK5105.887.M328 2006
  006.7'876--dc22

                                2005028126

British Library Cataloguing-in-Publication Data
A catalogue record for this book is available from the British Library.

ISBN 13: 978-1-138-14598-6 (hbk)
ISBN 13: 978-0-240-80754-6 (pbk)

Table of Contents

Chapter 1: Quick Start

Chapter 2: Basic Webcasting Concepts

Chapter 3: Digital Audio and Video Basics

Chapter 4: Business Considerations

Chapter 5: Choosing the Right Partners

Chapter 6: Webcast Production Planning

Chapter 7: Webcast Audio Production

Chapter 8: Webcast Video Production

Chapter 9: Webcast Encoding

Chapter 10: Webcast Authoring

Chapter 11: Webcast Distribution

Chapter 12: Case Studies

Acknowledgments

The process of webcasting has come a long way since the first webcasts took place in 1994 and 1995. Back then, specific hardware and software tools did not exist. A webcaster had to be knowledgeable about all facets of the process and many times they often knew more about some things, for instance ISDN lines, than the person installing them. In the early days, webcasting truly was an art that required not only a wide knowledge base but also a love for the medium, as no one was making money on webcasting.

Today, the process is much simpler, with many tools and vendors available to choose from. Business models exist to position webcasters for success. Hardware products, encoding tools and connectivity advances have made the process more reliable and its use in every vertical industry is a testament to its mass-market appeal.

Every webcast that takes place, large or small, includes a team of production people. Over the past ten years, Steve and I have had the privilege and opportunity to work with many very talented webcasters who were responsible for helping to bring this medium to fruition. While we can't list them all, some of the early webcasters in the industry who deserve credit are Jerry Black, Chris Kelly, Jonathan Troen, Ben Johnson, Eric Magnuson, Ross McFarlane, Christopher Levy, Cory Smith, Pat Greer, John Engel, Marc Scarpa, Jake Solomon, Halley Bock, Martin Tobias, Mike Schrock, John Luini, Zane Vella, Chris Otto, Dan Lieberman, William Mutual, Brad Pumphrey, Michael Ahern and many others.

We would also like to gratefully acknowledge the entire staff at Focal Press, who have been patient and helpful throughout the writing process. In particular, we'd like to thank Joanne Tracy, Angelina Ward, Howard Jones, Rachel Epstein, and Becky Golden-Harrell.

For Steve and I, this book has truly been a work in the making from our first webcasts through the thousands of webcasts we've had a hand in. For the past ten years, we've both spent countless hours on the road, in airports, in foreign countries and at event locations literally in the middle of nowhere learning, improvising, and improving the process of webcasting. For both of us, this first decade of webcasting has been fueled by a love for what we do. We hope you enjoy webcasting as much as we do.

About the Authors

Steve Mack

Steve Mack has spent the last ten years at the forefront of the streaming media industry. He is a principal at LUX Media (*http://luxmedia.com*), a firm specializing in interactive media design, including large-scale live event production, a/v production, authoring, encoding, hardware and software implementation, training, original music composition, and script writing. Through its 501 division, LUX also offers hosting and consulting services targeted at progressive non-profit organizations.

An accomplished author, Steve wrote *The Streaming Media Bible* (Wiley, Spring 2002), the de-facto standard text on the subject, as well as an article for the *Encyclopedia of Electrical and Electronics Engineering* entitled "Broadcasting on the Internet" (Wiley, 1999).

Steve has produced some of the largest and most prestigious Internet broadcasts, including U2 live from Notre Dame (Yahoo Internet Magazine's "Top of the Net for 2001"), the ACLU 2004 Members Conference, the Rolling Stones Bridges to Babylon tour, Elton John's Oscar Party, as well as the WOMAD, Bumbershoot, South by Southwest, and Tibetan Freedom Festivals, The New York Digital Club Festivals, the MTV Europe Awards, President Clinton's second inaugural address, and the first ever public live Internet broadcast of a Seattle Mariners game in 1995.

Steve is a popular and sought-after public speaker, having presented and given workshops internationally at the National Association of Broadcasters, Internet World, the Mayo Clinic, the X-Media Lab in Sydney, Australia, the RealConference, Streaming Media East and West, and South by Southwest. He also chaired the Internet Audio Workshop at the 105th Audio Engineering Society conference.

Previously at RealNetworks for five years (*http://www.real.com*) as Executive Producer of New Programming and Special Events, Steve worked with high-profile customers and partners to create cutting-edge programming and presentations. Prior to this, Steve managed the RealNetworks Media Lab, where he oversaw the team responsible for the majority of content created for the RealNetworks websites.

Steve is a board member of the Northwest Chapter of the Recording Academy, a member of the Audio Engineering Society, and one of the organizing founders of No Vote Left Behind, a political action committee rallying the musical community in Seattle, Washington. He volunteers for the Northwest Environment Watch, a non-profit organization dedicated to a sustainable economy in the Pacific Northwest, and in his spare time maintains the Harry Shearer website.

Before his current career in interactive media, Steve was a professional musician traveling the world and releasing five albums' worth of material with critically acclaimed Irish rock group That Petrol Emotion. During this time he built, owned, and operated Bang Bang Studios in London, England, a commercial 24-track recording studio where he produced and engineered hundreds of releases. He is still active in the music industry as a producer/engineer and solo performer.

Dan Rayburn

Dan Rayburn is recognized as the "voice for the streaming media industry" and as one of the Internet industry's foremost authorities, speakers, and writers on Streaming and Digital Media Technologies for the past ten years.

He is Executive Vice President for StreamingMedia.com, a diversified news media company with a mission to serve and educate the streaming media industry and corporations adopting Internet based audio and video technology. Its website (*www.StreamingMedia.com*), print magazine, research reports and tradeshows are considered the premier destinations for professionals seeking industry news, articles, white papers, directories and tutorials.

Prior to StreamingMedia.com, he founded a streaming media services division for the Globix Corporation, a publicly traded NASDAQ company, which became one of the largest global streaming media service providers specializing in on-site event production for webcasts around the world. Prior to Globix, he co-founded one of the industry's first streaming media webcasting production companies, Live On Line, successfully acquired by Digital Island for $70 million dollars.

An established writer, Mr. Rayburn's articles on streaming media trends and technologies have been translated into four languages and are regularly published in major trade magazines and web portals around the world. He is co-author of the first business focused book on the industry, *The Business of Streaming & Digital Media*. Regularly consulted by the media for insight into business trends and technology, Mr. Rayburn has been featured in over one hundred print and on-line articles.

Mr. Rayburn also consults for corporations who are implementing digital media services and products in the broadcast, wireless, IPTV, security and cable industries. Over the past ten years he has helped develop, consult, and implement streaming media solutions for prestigious companies in the enterprise, entertainment and government sectors including webcasts for A&E, ABC, Apple, Atlantic Records, American Express, BMG, BP, CBS, Cisco, Elektra, Excite.com, HBO, House Of Blues, ifilm, Indy 500, Intel, ITN, KPMG, Microsoft, MTV, Pepsi, Price Waterhouse Coopers, Qualcomm, RealNetworks, Sony Music, Twentieth Century Fox, United Nations, Viacom, VH1 and Warner Brothers among others.

Mr. Rayburn travels internationally as a featured industry expert and is sought out to speak on the current and future direction of streaming media technology, trends and business cases. A current technology advisor to many universities in the US, he has also taught Internet Broadcasting classes at New York University (NYU) and regularly lectures at numerous academic institutions.

Introduction

There's something about a live event that captures the imagination, whether it's the final round of a sporting event or a special performance by a popular musical act. These days, you're likely to see both during the same broadcast. So it's no surprise that as soon as streaming media technology was developed, people wanted to broadcast live events on the Internet. While there are some arguments on what the word *webcast* means, most people typically refer to webcasting or cybercasting as a *live* stream on the Internet.

Initially most Internet broadcasts, or *webcasts*, consisted of entertainment or sporting events. The impetus was to generate buzz by producing the "largest" webcast to date, as each subsequent press release gleefully announced even if there was no business logic behind it. However, as the technology has matured and the initial fascination evolved, webcasting is being used for more practical purposes, such as investor calls, CEO addresses, religious ceremonies, and terrestrial radio simulcasts.

Webcasts can include audio, video, and other data types such as PowerPoint slides, animation, or whiteboard-type applications and are typically referred to as an *interactive webcasts* when such components exist. Many webcasts also include some form of communication between the audience and the talent. This is one of the advantages that webcasting has over traditional forms of broadcast. There are a number of others:

- **Lower Cost of Entry**: Webcasting does not require a multimillion dollar infrastructure
- **Unlimited Spectrum**: Webcasting is not currently regulated by any governmental agency and does not require a license
- **Not Limited by Geography**: Webcasting can be local or international
- **Can be Targeted**: Webcasting can be cost-effective for smaller audiences

Webcasting also has some limitations:

- **Smaller audiences**: The Internet is not yet capable of sustaining audience sizes that rival traditional TV broadcasts
- **Incremental cost per viewer**: Bandwidth costs money, and each additional viewer adds to this cost compared to a terrestrial broadcast where the volume of users does not increase the cost
- **Quality**: Though technically possible, broadcast-quality webcasts are not yet a reality

Despite the limitations of webcasting, there are still many situations where webcasting makes good financial sense. Many large scale enterprises realize this and are actively deploying webcasting as a cost-cutting exercise for internal and external purposes. Educational institutions use webcasting as an integral part of their distance learning courses. Non-profit organizations are using webcasts to reach and expand their membership.

So how are webcasts produced? Essentially a webcast combines traditional broadcasting practice with streaming media technology. On the broadcast side, solid audio and video engineering practice is applied to produce a high quality source signal. However, instead of sending the signal to a broadcast tower, it is fed into a streaming media encoding system, and then sent to streaming media servers for distribution on the Internet.

Producing a webcast is basically the same process as creating an on-demand streaming media file. Webcasting, however, is a little trickier because there is no room for error. Webcasts are produced in real-time; this affects each stage of the streaming media process. But with a little forethought and a lot of planning, a successful webcast is well within your reach.

Successful Webcast Ingredients

The webcasting process is the same as creating on-demand streaming media files, with the important addition of a planning phase:

- **Planning**: Justifying the costs, securing the location, tools, and crew
- **Production**: Capturing the raw audio and video feeds, any other data types
- **Encoding**: Converting the raw media into formats that can be streamed
- **Authoring**: Connecting the audience to the webcast via a link on a web page
- **Distribution**: Securing the infrastructure to distribute the streams

Each phase has unique requirements during a webcast. The most important thing to remember is that you only get one shot at a webcast. If something goes wrong, the webcast may grind to a halt if you haven't planned appropriately. Bearing this in mind, the planning phase becomes paramount, and the key to all other phases can be summed up in a single word: redundancy.

Planning is the key to a successful webcast. There's only one chance to get it right, so everything must be in place well before the webcast begins. The right tools, sufficient personnel, a robust streaming architecture, and plenty of bandwidth all must be provisioned in advance. Once everything is in place, each and every component must be thoroughly tested.

First, check out the proposed location for the webcast. Does it have enough power? Is there room enough for your equipment? Is there enough light? Are the acoustics suitable? Is there Internet connectivity on site? How will you get your feed to the streaming media servers?

For the production phase, a full complement of audio and video gear is needed to create a broadcast quality stream, including backups in case of failure. It's crucial to have extra microphones, cameras, mixing desks, and anything else needed to produce the webcast.

Bring extra encoding hardware for encoding redundancy. At least one backup encoding machine is required, more if you're encoding multiple bit rates or formats. If you can afford it, you should also invest in redundant connectivity—the broadcast will grind to a halt if the connectivity disappears.

A robust streaming server infrastructure is required to handle the demands of the projected audience. Bandwidth requirements increase dramatically during a webcast, as does the load on the servers. Depending on the streaming platform you're using, you may have licensing restrictions on the number of streams you're capable of broadcasting simultaneously.

Make sure you have enough personnel and good lines of communication. Webcasts are far too complex for small crews to pull off. You need individuals responsible for each and every aspect of the broadcast, and they need to be able to communicate with everyone else involved in the webcast.

Finally, the importance of testing cannot be stressed enough. Test the connectivity on site well before the broadcast. Test the production equipment before the broadcast begins, preferably the day before the broadcast. Test the encoding equipment and load-test the streaming media infrastructure. Test the links on the website, and have as many people as possible participate in a dry-run of the webcast. The only way to minimize the chance of failure is to test as much as possible before the actual event.

Producing webcasts to a high quality standard is an involved process. A number of different skill sets are involved, and there is a significant amount of risk. However, broken down into its component parts, webcasting is not rocket science. There is no reason you shouldn't be able to pull off a successful webcast provided you give yourself enough lead time. Producing a webcast, especially on a small scale is not as hard and difficult as people make it out to be and this book will help assist you in making it even easier.

How to Use This Book

This book is organized roughly in the order which a webcast is executed, and divided into chapters that correspond to the different components of a webcast. Chapters generally start with a conceptual overview and get more detailed as they go on. Though the webcasting process is a continuum, each chapter is relatively self-contained, so feel free to jump directly to a chapter that addresses your area of interest.

Organization

The book begins with a Quick Start, which shows you just how simple webcasting can be. If you want to start webcasting immediately, start here.

Chapters 2 and 3 provide some background about streaming media and digital audio and video. If you've never worked with digital audio or video before, or need some background about what streaming media is and how it is created, you'll find a good overview here.

Chapters 4 and 5 are focused on the business of webcasting. Before planning a webcast, a frank discussion about the legal and financial implications must be had. These chapters discuss the legal intricacies of a webcast, along with expected costs and revenues. Partnering opportunities are also discussed. Many webcasts are produced by a number of companies working together, similar to the traditional broadcast world.

Chapters 6 through 8 deal with webcast production practice. To a large extent this is where the heart of the book lies, because this is where webcasting differs from creating standard streaming media files. Planning, equipment, crew requirements, connectivity, and audio and video production techniques can be found here.

Chapters 9 and 10 cover encoding and authoring best practices. There are a number of concerns you need to take into account such as the scale of the webcast, and other concerns such as bandwidth and hosting costs. This section also covers how to author simple metafiles and HTML pages with embedded players and how to ensure that the method you use scales properly during large events.

Chapter 11 is concerned with distribution, which is obviously the key to a successful webcast. This section discusses how to plan and implement a redundant server infrastructure, and how to estimate what your infrastructure needs are.

Finally, there are a number of case studies, both successful and not so successful. These case studies provide you with some real-life examples of how webcasts are planned and executed, how they were justified, what went right, and possibly more important, what went wrong.

Sidebars

There are three types of sidebars used in this book: "Author Tip," "Inside the Industry," and "Alert." Each is separated from the text and gives you quick, helpful information that is easy to find.

 Author Tip: Gives tips that are directly from the author's experience in the field.

 Inside the Industry: Relays information about companies, behind the scenes happenings, quotes from people in the industry, a bit from a case study, statistics, market research, anything to do with the topic's industry that doesn't necessarily come from the author's experience.

 Alert: Spells out important information such as technical considerations, troubleshooting, warning of potential pitfalls, and anything else that needs special attention.

A Quick Word about Platforms

While there are open standards in the world of Internet streaming (most notably the MPEG standards), the reality is that there are a number of streaming systems out there, and very little true interoperability. While those of us in the industry would love to see a universal standard, there are good reasons it has yet to happen, and there is little chance that it is going to happen soon.

This book tries to be as even-handed as possible in its treatment of the different streaming systems, and endeavors not to recommend any particular system. Each platform has its advantages and disadvantages, which should be carefully considered in the planning phase of your webcast.

This book can not possibly cover every possible webcast topic, but should give you a firm understanding of the technologies involved, and the planning that is required for a successful webcast. Although the technology and infrastructure are still evolving, the information in this book should remain relevant for some time.

Webcasts are exciting, and with adequate planning, even fun. Just remember the cardinal rules:

- Take the time to plan appropriately
- Keep it simple
- Bring two of everything
- Be kind to your distribution partner(s)
- Start early

Welcome to the world of webcasting.

Support: We're Here to Help

While this book's aim is to be easy to follow, further follow-up questions and feedback are welcomed at any time. We'd love to hear from you, even if it's just to request more statistics, be added to our mailing list, or have any streaming and digital media related questions answered. If you are looking for insight on new service offerings, a recommended service provider, or have questions regarding your webcasting implementations, we'd be glad to answer them. You can reach us directly at:

help@webcastingbook.com
(917) 523-4562

CHAPTER 1

Quick Start

Instructors always want students to understand the theoretical basis of what they're teaching because that's the type of knowledge that sticks. Pushing buttons in a prescribed order is the type of thing that you forget. However, students don't learn if they aren't excited. Bearing that in mind, this chapter is for those of you who can't wait to get your fingers on the buttons.

It's time to roll up your sleeves and fire up your first webcast. This chapter offers a *tiny* bit of background, and covers:

- Getting Ready for a Webcast
- Your First Webcast

Getting Ready for a Webcast

Webcasts run smoothly if and only if they are adequately planned and prepared. With proper preparation, any minor problems that arise can be solved quickly and simply. Ninety-five percent of the work involved in a webcast is done before the actual event.

Since this is only an exercise and not an actual broadcast, no planning is involved. It's instructive, however, to go through the process to see what's involved in an actual broadcast.

Business Considerations

If this was an actual webcast, you'd want to find out who the audience is, whether the webcast is absolutely necessary, and how much it will cost to produce. This could be balanced against the perceived return, whether financial or goodwill.

In this instance, the audience (you) is very excited about this webcast. It's absolutely necessary that it be live. The cost is relatively low, and the return is projected to be an unbridled enthusiasm to read the rest of this book. So in this case, a live webcast is justified.

The first thing to do is to start planning. The way to plan for a webcast is to consider every step of the webcast process and figure out what is needed. You're going to need equipment, software, crew, and Internet connectivity.

Planning for your Webcast

The webcasting process can be divided into five steps. In this instance, some things have been taken care of for you, but it's instructive to note the planning process, since every webcast you plan will replicate it, if only on a larger scale.

Production is where the bulk of your equipment and crew requirements are. You need enough of both to successfully execute the webcast, along with spare equipment and crew—just in case.

Equipment You'll Need — At the very least, you're going to need an audio and a video source. For the purposes of this chapter, you can encode off a CD, a webcam, or anything that provides you with audio and/or video.

For an actual webcast, you'd need enough audio and video equipment to produce a broadcast quality signal. This equipment can be purchased, rented, or hired from a third-party production house. You can hire third parties to produce the audio and video for you. For now, figure out what your source is going to be, and have it nearby.

Computer Hardware You'll Need — Thankfully, most multimedia computers these days have enough horsepower to run webcasting software. However, most computers do not come with a video capture card, so if you want to encode a video stream, you're going to need either a video capture card or an external video capture unit.

Software You'll Need — Each of the major streaming platforms has software to *encode* the webcast. Encoding is converting the raw audio and video feeds into formats that can be streamed across a network. For this exercise, you'll need the Windows Media Encoder and the Windows Media Player installed.

If you do not have these already installed, both are available as free downloads from the Microsoft website (*http://www.microsoft.com/windowsmedia*).

Inside the Industry

Mac vs. PC

Unfortunately, there is currently no Windows Media Encoder for live broadcasting on the Mac. Mac users may therefore feel slightly short-changed by this chapter. Now is as good a time as any to address this issue.

While this book attempts to be as platform-agnostic as possible, the reality is that there are a number of cross-platform issues. The purpose of this chapter is to illustrate the webcasting process as quickly and simply as possible, for the largest percentage of the audience.

The rest of this book uses examples from a variety of streaming media platforms. Windows Media was chosen for this chapter because:

- The ubiquity of the Windows platform

- The tools are free

- There is no free QuickTime live encoding tool

- There is no free, simple Flash live encoding tool

Throughout the book a number of streaming technologies will be showcased. Occasionally cross-platform issues will arise. For the most part, however, the information in this book is high-level and applicable to any webcasting application.

Encoding Planning — For this exercise we'll encode a single stream, in a single format, to a single server. We're going to encode this stream at a moderate *bit rate*, which determines the quality of the video and the Internet connection required to watch the stream. Don't worry too much about the terminology at this point; all this will be covered in more detail later on in the book.

It is worth remembering, though, that for an actual webcast the audience should be considered, and formats and bit rates chosen accordingly. You may need to provide streams in a number of formats, and at varying bit rates. This would impact the amount of computer hardware required.

Authoring Planning — For the purposes of this exercise you will be linking directly to the stream. However, for an actual broadcast you'd need to consider what method you'd be using to showcase your stream. Will it be rendered in a pop-up player or embedded in a web page? Will a software load balancer be needed?

Distribution Planning — The projected audience size directly impacts the amount of distribution you require. Small webcasts may utilize only a single streaming server; large webcasts may use large, geographically distributed server farms. It's important to work with your network administrators and/or your streaming service provider to figure out how to satisfy your distribution needs.

Crew Planning — Many small companies have small multimedia departments that handle all the company's media needs. A single person might be in charge of shooting video, editing, encoding, and posting files to the servers. This isn't possible during a webcast, because everything happens simultaneously.

The preceding few pages should give you an idea of the type of planning that is required for a webcast. In reality there are many more things to consider, for instance legal issues, transportation, and many others. The key is to start early. For actual webcasts, the planning should begin the day the webcast is suggested and run right up until the webcast goes live.

Your First Webcast

Now that you've persevered through the background part of this chapter, it's finally time for your first webcast. You'll be encoding and distributing a live stream from a single computer and testing it to make sure it is working. Regardless of what software platform you're working on, or how large your webcast is, this is the basic architecture of every webcast (see **Figure 1-1**).

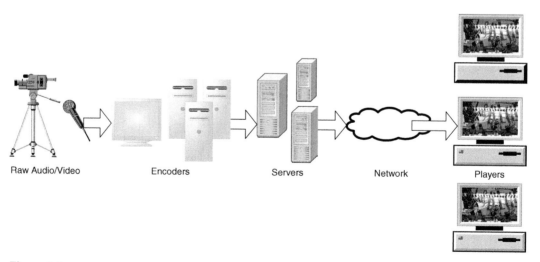

Raw Audio/Video   Encoders   Servers   Network   Players

Figure 1-1
The basic signal flow of a webcast.

Moving from left to right, we can follow the signal flow:

1. Audio and/or video sources are plugged into an encoding computer.

2. The encoding computer converts the raw audio and video feeds into a format that can be streamed across the network.

3. The encoding computer either hands off the live stream to a streaming server on the same machine, or sends it across a network to a streaming server.

4. The server receives the incoming live stream, for eventual delivery to the audience.

5. Player software on the audience's computer connects to the streaming server, and requests the webcast.

6. The server delivers the live stream to the player, which plays it back on the viewer's computer.

That's it in a nutshell. In this case, we're going to do the encoding and the distribution from the same machine. The Windows Media Encoder can also function as a streaming server. While it does not have any of the advanced functionality of Windows Media Services (the Windows Media distribution platform), it can distribute a live stream directly to Windows Media Players. Let's get started.

Connect Your Sources

The first thing you have to do is connect the audio and video sources to the encoding computer. Connect the camera to the video capture card, or plug in a webcam if that's all you've got. Connect the audio source to the sound card input.

Be sure to use the correct inputs. Microphones should be plugged into the mic input on the sound card; any other audio source should be plugged into the line level input. If the video card has multiple inputs, make a note of which input you're using—you may need to configure your video capture card application to select the correct input.

Set Up the Encoding Software

Open up the Windows Media Encoder. If it's the first time you've used the Windows Media Encoder, a wizard opens up offering you a number of choices (see **Figure 1-2**). If this window does not appear, click the "New Session" button in the top left of the Windows Media Encoder.

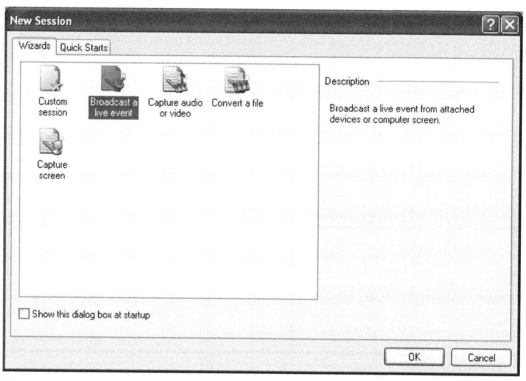

Figure 1-2
The Windows Media Encoder New Session window.

From here, the Windows Media Encoder walks you through the steps to set up your broadcast:

1. Select the "Broadcast a Live Event" icon, and click Okay. This brings up the Device Options window (see **Figure 1-3**).

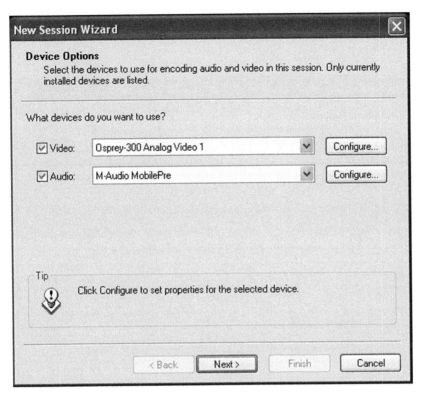

Figure 1-3
The Device Options window.

2.   Select your audio and video sources from the Video and Audio drop down menus in the Device Options window. Unless there are multiple devices installed, the Windows Media Encoder defaults to the right settings. Click the Next button.

3. Select "Pull from the encoder" from the Broadcast Method window (see **Figure 1-4**). Click the Next button.

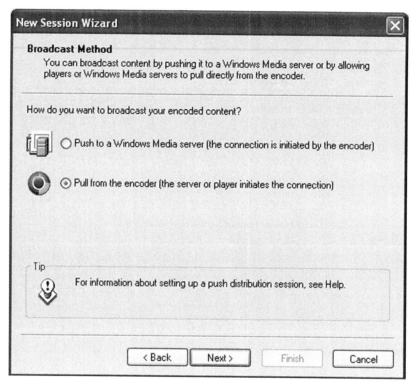

Figure 1-4
The Broadcast Method window.

4. Enter a port for the broadcast connection on this page (see **Figure 1-5**). The default is 8080, which should work for most applications. Click the Next button.

ALERT If you're behind a *firewall*, which is a software or hardware device designed to protect your network from intruders, people outside of your network may not be able to see your webcast. Firewall issues are solved by either choosing a port that your firewall allows traffic on, or opening a specific port on the firewall for streaming traffic.

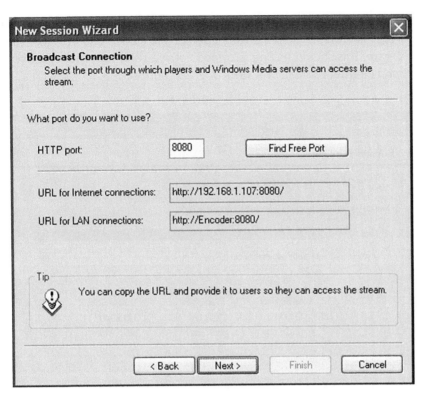

Figure 1-5
The Broadcast Connection window.

Author's Tip

If you're doing an audio only broadcast, the default bit rate is 135 Kbps. This is also fine for broadband connections. Choose a lower bit rate if you're on a slower Internet connection such as a dial-up modem. In this case you should choose a bit rate of approximately 20–30 Kbps.

5.　Choose the encoding settings from the Encoding Options window (see **Figure 1-6**). The Windows Media Encoder defaults to a 282 Kbps CBR (constant bit rate) stream. This should be fine, provided both you and your audience have broadband Internet connections. Click the Next button.

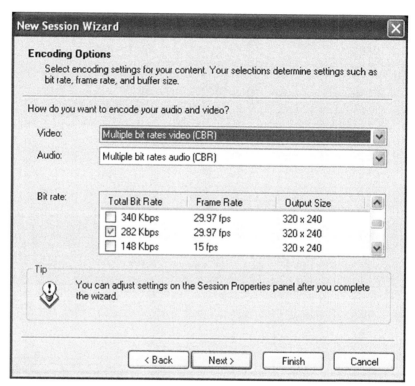

Figure 1-6
The Encoding Options window.

6. The next screen offers the option to archive the webcast to a local drive (see **Figure 1-7**). Leave this option de-selected, and click the Next button.

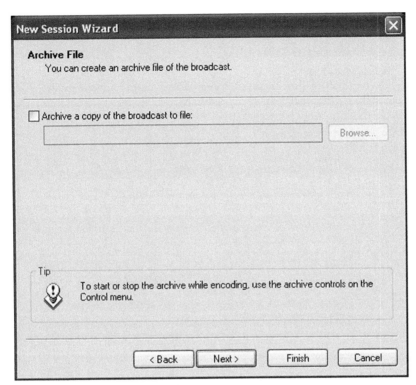

Figure 1-7
The Archive File window.

7.   The next screen offers the option to include additional files in your presentation (see **Figure 1-8**). For this exercise, select the "No, I want to encode from my selected devices only" option, and click the Next button.

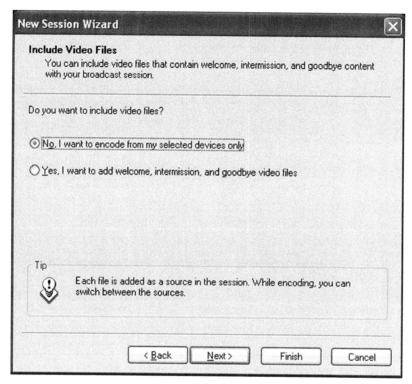

Figure 1-8
The Include Video Files window.

8.   Enter title, author, and copyright information on the next screen (see **Figure 1-9**). Click the Next button.

9.   The final screen provides an opportunity for you to review all the information you just entered. Make sure the "Begin broadcasting when I click finish" checkbox is checked (see **Figure 1-10**), and click the Finish button.

After you click the Finish button, the Windows Media Encoder will start encoding the stream. You should see the words "Encoder broadcasting" along the bottom of the Windows Media Encoder interface, as well as green bars crawling across a progress bar.

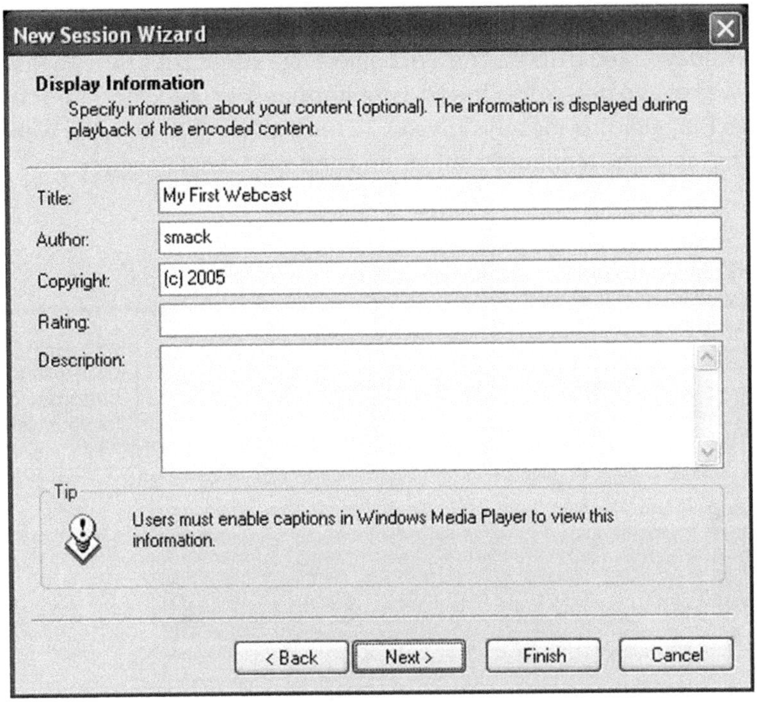

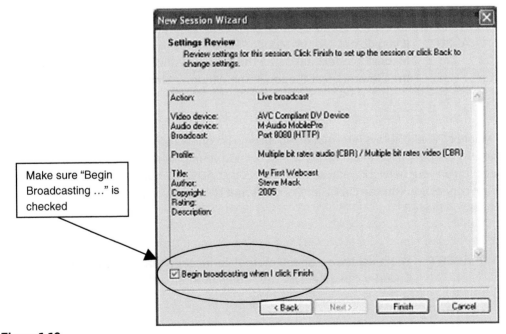

Figure 1-9
The Display Information window.

Figure 1-10
The Settings Review window.

Test the Webcast

Now that the Windows Media Encoder is encoding a live stream, it's time to test the webcast. But first, we have to determine the URL (uniform resource locator) for the stream. The Windows Media Encoder provides this for you. To find out the URL for your webcast, click on the Connections tab in the Monitor Panel of the Windows Media Encoder.

When players connect to your webcast, they are listed in the Direct Connections section.

Click on one of these buttons to copy the URL for your webcast.

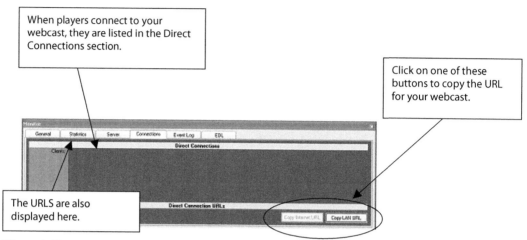

The URLS are also displayed here.

Figure 1-11
The Connections tab of the Monitor panel offers useful information about your webcast.

 ALERT If you do not see the Monitor Panel in the lower half of the Windows Media Encoder, make sure the Monitor Panel option is selected from the View menu at the top of the Windows Media Encoder.

The Monitor Panel displays information about who is connected to your webcast, as well as the URL for people connecting inside and outside your local network. For people connecting on your network, you can click the "Copy LAN URL" button. If you have a direct Internet connection you can click the "Copy Internet URL" button. The URLs are also displayed on the left.

 ALERT You must have a direct Internet connection that the Windows Media Encoder can detect for the "Copy Internet URL" to function.

If you want to test your broadcast from another machine, click the "Copy LAN URL" or "Copy Internet URL" button to copy the address of the webcast. Paste the link into an email and send it to the other machine. Alternatively you can write down the address shown on the left side of the Monitor Panel.

Open up the Windows Media Player on the other machine, and from the file menu, choose "Open URL" (or simply press Ctrl + U). Enter the URL from the Windows Media Encoder.

Click okay. It may take a few moments for the Windows Media Player to connect to the encoder. Once it does, the Windows Media Player buffers the stream, and begins playback. At this point, your webcast is live. Congratulations.

If you wave at the camera, you'll notice that the live stream is slightly behind. This is because both Windows Media Encoder and Player buffer a few seconds of the broadcast to ensure smooth playback. This delay can be minimized, but never completely eliminated. It's currently built-in to all webcasting architectures.

You have now set up your first webcast. Audio and video sources were connected to a computer that encoded the signal into a streaming media format. This stream was then distributed to players, in this case via the serving ca-

Author's Tip

If you're testing the webcast on the same machine as you're encoding, you may have to use the following syntax:

http://localhost:{port}

where {port} is the port number you chose in step 4.

Author's Tip

You can distribute this link via email, or on a webpage. In most cases you won't want to distribute this raw link—you'll want to create a metafile, and you'll want to use multiple servers to distribute the load. However, for testing purposes this link will work just fine.

pabilities of the Windows Media Encoder. Everything that follows in this book will be based on this simple architecture, except that for large scale webcasts we'll be using a streaming media server for distribution. Keeping this architecture in mind will enable you to understand as things become more complex to handle the real world load of a public webcast.

Conclusion

Webcasting is a simple process built from three basic ingredients: encoders, servers, and players. Webcasting becomes complex as the audience becomes larger. Webcasts can be expensive to produce, so be sure the proposed webcast satisfies the 5 W's (Who/What/Where/Why/When). The next chapter is a high-level overview of the webcasting process, and introduces the concepts and language that are used throughout the remainder of the book.

CHAPTER 2

Basic Webcasting Concepts

Webcasting combines a number of different disciplines, such as audio and video engineering, web page authoring, and server administration. Like many other technical fields, it also has its own jargon. When you're trying to put a webcast together it's helpful to understand how the different disciplines work together, and what the crew is talking about.

This chapter provides an overview of the mechanics of streaming media, which is the technology that webcasting is built on, as well as a look at the tools, technologies, and jargon used during a webcast. Specifically this chapter covers:

- Streaming Media: What It Is and How It Works
- The Importance of Bandwidth
- Webcasting System Components
- The Webcasting Process
- Webcasting Tools
- Platform Considerations

Streaming Media: What It Is and How It Works

Webcasting is a specialized application of streaming media technology. Streaming media enables real time delivery of media presentations across a network. Streaming media technology is similar to the technology used to deliver web pages, but with a key difference— web servers *download* files, whereas streaming media servers *stream* files.

Downloaded files are displayed, or *rendered* only after the entire file has been delivered and reassembled. Streamed files are played back as they are delivered (see **Figure 2-1**). For very small media files, the difference may not be noticeable. For larger files, however, streaming media offer a number of advantages:

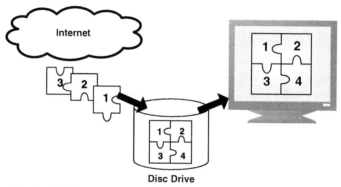

a. Downloaded files are reassembled, then displayed.

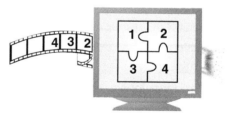

b. Streaming files are played back as they arrive and then discarded.

Figure 2-1
Downloading is different than streaming.

- **Real-time**: Streaming media files begin playback after a few seconds, rather than after the entire file has been delivered.
- **Control/Interactivity**: Streaming media enables viewers to control and interact with the presentation.
- **Security**: Streaming media is played back and discarded instead of being stored on the user's hard drive.
- **Live broadcasting**: Perhaps most importantly, streaming media enables live broadcasts, or *webcasts*.

Some short on-demand media files are delivered using a hybrid technology known as *progressive download*. Progressive download files are delivered by a web server, but playback begins before the entire file has been delivered.

Depending on the size of the file, playback may begin anywhere from immediately to a few minutes after the file has been requested. While this is an improvement over pure download, it is still limited in its applications. It is fine for short files such as movie trailers or advertisements. For all other media delivery, streaming is a much better approach.

It should be obvious that there is no such thing as a live download, progressive or otherwise. Webcasting requires streaming technology, because it happens in real time. Webcasting also requires that you understand the concept of bandwidth.

The Importance of Bandwidth

Bandwidth refers to the concurrent capacity of an Internet connection—the greater the capacity, the higher the bandwidth. Bandwidth is generally measured in bits per second (bps). The bandwidths of typical internet connections are listed in **Table 2-1**.

Table 2-1
Typical Internet bandwidths.

Connection Type	Bandwidth/Bit rate
Dial-up (56K Modem)	34–37 Kilobits per second (Kbps)
Broadband (Cable, xDSL)	200–1000 Kbps
Frame Relay, Fractional T-1	128 Kbps–1.5 Megabits per second (Mbps)
T-1	1.5 Mbps
Ethernet	10 Mbps
T-3	45 Mbps

These measurements represent the maximum theoretical capacities. Actual capacities can be far less.

Bandwidth is important in a number of ways during a webcast:

- The bandwidth of individual audience members determines how the webcast should be encoded
- The bandwidth available on site determines how much data can be sent to the distribution servers
- The aggregate bandwidth used determines the bandwidth charge

Each of these has an impact on a webcast, and must be taken into consideration. Bandwidth is a recurring issue during a webcast, and is discussed in more detail throughout the book as it pertains to each particular topic.

Webcasting System Components

Webcasts vary in size and complexity, but at their core they are very simple. No matter how large or small, all webcasts are assembled using three basic building blocks: encoders, servers, and players (see **Figure 2-2**).

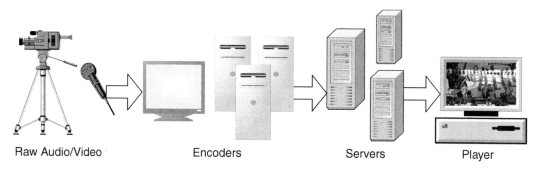

Raw Audio/Video   Encoders   Servers   Player

Figure 2-2
The basic flow of a webcast.

Encoders, Servers, and Players

Working from left to right in **Figure 2-2**, the first component of a webcast is the *encoder*. The encoder converts the raw audio and video signals into a format that can be streamed across a network. They are necessary because the data rates of raw audio and video are far too high for network delivery. Encoders are covered in more detail in Chapter 9.

The next component is the *server*. Streaming media servers receive the incoming encoded streams from encoders, and then distribute them to the audience. They may also distribute them to other servers, for *load balancing* and redundancy purposes. Load balancing is a technique where a number of servers are used to distribute a webcast to improve performance and reliability. Servers are covered in more detail in Chapter 11, Webcast Distribution.

The final component in a webcast is the player. The player communicates with the streaming media server, receives the incoming encoded stream, and renders it. It also provides the viewer with control over the playback of the stream. Different streaming media players may offer different features, but they all provide the same basic functionality.

Large-scale webcast architectures are more complex, but are comprised of the same basic building blocks. Because redundancy is key to any webcast, multiple encoders and multiple servers are used, and of course the audience may include hundreds or thousands of players (see **Figure 2-3**).

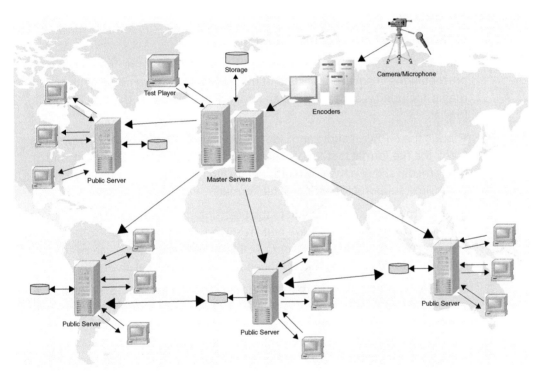

Figure 2-3
Large scale, redundant webcast infrastructures are built from the same three components.

Protocols, File Formats, and Codecs
It's not enough to have an encoder, a server, and a player. To be useful, the three components must be able to communicate and interact with each other. To this end, standardized protocols, file formats, and codecs have been developed.

Protocols determine how components communicate. For example, when you type a website location into your browser, it begins with "*http://*." This stands for hypertext transfer protocol, which is the protocol web servers and browsers use. Streaming servers use a variety of protocols, the most common being RTSP (real time streaming protocol).

Once information has been exchanged via a standardized protocol, the applications need to know how the data is arranged. This is determined by the file format. A file format generally consists of a *header* which contains information about the file, followed by the audio and video data. There may also be additional *tracks* included in the file that contain information about the layout of the presentation, special effects, or closed caption text.

Most streaming media platforms use proprietary file formats, which is why files created for one format may not play back in another player. The notable exceptions to this are MPEG files, which use a standardized file format.

Inside the Industry

 MPEG-4—File Format of the Future?

The MPEG-4 standard defines a broad framework for creating interactive media presentations. A small subsection of the MPEG-4 standard pertains to streaming media. Included is a file format standard, which is based on the QuickTime file format.

Though the MPEG-4 audio and video codecs are the focus of much development, the file format is still not widely in use. RealNetworks, Microsoft, and Macromedia still use their own proprietary file formats. Unsurprisingly, only QuickTime supports the MPEG-4 file format.

Some of this was previously due to the licensing issues surrounding MPEG-4, but for the most part these have been resolved. (For the most up-to-date licensing details visit *www.m4if.org*.) At this point the problem is companies' reluctance to do anything that might endanger their market share.

Because most streaming formats are already moving to the RTSP protocol, a standardized file format would arguably be of most use to the streaming media community, since it's a major hurdle to interoperability. Standardized codecs would also be useful, but until recently the standardized MPEG-4 codecs were simply not in the same league as the video codecs available from Microsoft and RealNetworks. This is rapidly changing.

MPEG-4 is seeing rapid adoption in the cell phone industry, where standards are absolutely necessary. Whether or not MPEG-4 ever becomes the standard for streaming media on desktops remains to be seen.

Finally, once the data has been exchanged, the streaming media player must decode the information so that it can be rendered. This is done using a *codec*. A codec (a contraction of **co**der-**dec**oder) is a set of rules that dictates how data is encoded and decoded. Codecs are necessary because raw audio and video files are far too large for network delivery.

Codecs are used by many applications. Most images on the Internet are encoded using either the JPG or GIF codecs. Archiving applications such as WinZip and StuffIt use codecs. Streaming media platforms use audio and video codecs, and others if other data types are being streamed.

ALERT Unfortunately, codecs are for the most part proprietary to each streaming media format. Files encoded in one format generally cannot be played in another format's player. This is partially due to the file format (as mentioned previously), and also due to the codec.

Streaming media companies are extremely protective of their codecs, because each new codec release generally represents a substantial leap in audio and video quality, and gives their platform a competitive edge.

The past few years, however, have seen less dramatic improvements. While some codecs are certainly better than others, the quality of all streaming media codecs is pretty good at this point. The decision as to which platform to use can be made without having to worry too much about which looks or sounds better.

Now that you know a little bit about the components of a webcasting system, it's time to find out how they all fit together.

The Webcasting Process

Creating streaming media is usually a four-step process: production, encoding, authoring, and distribution. When creating streaming media archives, these steps can be followed sequentially. However, during a webcast everything happens at the same time. This means you need enough equipment and crew to do four things at once. And therefore, to ensure a webcast runs smoothly, a crucial step must be added: planning.

Planning

Without proper planning, the chances of a successful webcast diminish drastically. Planning begins the moment a webcast is suggested, and continues up to the moment the webcast goes live.

Planning begins with the business issues as discussed in chapter 4. Webcasts are expensive to produce because of the increased equipment, crew, and bandwidth requirements. Therefore before too much time and effort is wasted a good business case must be made for the proposed webcast.

Once a webcast has been justified financially, planning for each step of the webcasting process can begin. Each step has its own set of requirements as you'll see in the subsequent sections. A detailed overview of the planning required for a webcast is covered in Chapters 4, 5, and 6.

Production

Production is the traditional side of a webcast, where cameras, microphones, and a host of other equipment are used to produce the audio and video signals. These may be combined with other elements such as PowerPoint slides, text, and animation to create the final presentation.

Production is particularly equipment-intensive; it also requires a lot of crew. In fact, production will always be the largest line item in your webcast budget, and is the reason why webcasting can be an expensive proposition. Much of this depends on the scale of your webcast. For example, webcasts of simple talking heads or audio-only events can be produced relatively cheaply. Webcast Production Best Practices are covered in Chapters 7 and 8.

Encoding

Encoding is where the raw audio and video feeds are converted into formats that can be delivered across a network. This is done either in software or hardware. The encoders must be connected to the Internet or whatever network you're webcasting on.

Encoding can either be done on-site at the event, or at the broadcast operations center (BOC) if you can send raw audio and video feeds back via satellite or a fiber connection. Smaller scale webcasts are encoded on site because of the significant cost savings over a satellite link. Larger scale webcasts may use both methods for redundancy. Webcast Encoding Best Practices are covered in Chapter 9.

Authoring

Authoring is how the audience is connected to the webcast. This can be as simple as a direct link sent via email, or a fancy presentation embedded in a webpage. It's generally a good idea to keep the authoring as simple as possible during a webcast. Webcast Authoring Best Practices are covered in Chapter 10.

Distribution

The final step of the webcasting process is distribution or delivery of the content. Small webcasts can easily be handled by a single streaming media server, but in general most webcasts use multiple servers for distribution. This is done for redundancy purposes, in case a server has trouble during a webcast.

Streaming servers operate differently than web servers, but from an administrative standpoint they can be treated in roughly the same manner. As long as they're up and running, the streaming server software takes care of the rest. Webcast Distribution is covered in Chapter 11.

Webcasting Tools

Each step of the webcasting process requires its own set of tools. As mentioned previously, the production phase is the most equipment intensive.

Production Tools

The amount of production equipment you need is directly related to the scale of your broadcast. You're going to need enough audio and video equipment to produce a high quality signal. Given the rapid advances in digital video and home recording technology, this need not be a crippling expense.

ALERT The most important thing to remember is that you must have a backup for each crucial link in the signal chain. That means at a minimum you should have a spare camera, a spare microphone, and plenty of spare cables. If you're bringing processing equipment, bring spares of those along as well.

If you're producing a fairly large webcast, it's probably a good idea to bring in a production partner. Not only will they have all the equipment that is needed to produce your event, but they'll assume responsibility for their part of the production, which reduces the amount of responsibility on your shoulders. Outsourcing vs. Do-It-Yourself is covered in Chapter 4.

Encoding Tools

To encode your webcast, you'll need enough machines to encode as many streams as you want to offer. There are encoding solutions that enable a single encoding machine to produce more than one live stream, but in general you'll need one encoder per stream. It's important to have spare encoders should any machines fail. At a minimum you'll want one spare machine, more if you're encoding multiple streams.

Author's Tip

There are a number of webcasting specialists who can deliver sturdy encoding solutions in flight cases, typically referred to in the industry as *road-encodes*.

The encoding machines must be equipped to handle the webcast. For example, if it is a video webcast, each encoding machine must have a video capture card. Most modern multimedia computers are more than capable of encoding a live stream, but even so there's no such thing as a computer that is too fast or has too much RAM. Get the best encoding machines you can afford.

Encoding is another part of the webcast that can be contracted out to a third party. If you're not going to be webcasting on a regular basis, you might consider outsourcing the encoding requirements.

Authoring Tools

Authoring can be done in a simple text application such as Notepad or using what-you-see-is-what-you-get (WYSIWYG) web page authoring tools. If you're creating a fancy presentation, you may need specialized authoring tools. In general this isn't a good idea, particularly if you need to change the presentation in an emergency. If you can't change your link quickly using a text editor, it's probably too complicated.

Distribution Tools

Finally, to distribute your webcast you'll need a robust streaming infrastructure. This consists of one or more servers running streaming media server applications. Streaming servers can run on their own or on the same box as other server applications.

After the webcast is finished, you'll want to gauge the success of your webcast by analyzing the streaming server log files. These provide you with a wealth of information including how many people viewed the webcast, how long they watched, and if there were any errors during the webcast.

Platform Considerations

One of the decisions you must make when planning a webcast is which technology you're going to use for distribution. As of 2005, the majority of all webcasts are done on the Windows Media and Real platforms, with QuickTime and Flash accounting for a smaller percentage.

Each platform has advantages and disadvantages that you'll have to consider. Amongst the questions to ask are:

- What operating system is the audience on, and what players are they likely to have already installed?
- Are there specialized data types or features of one particular platform that you want to use?
- Are licensing fees an issue?

Most of the streaming media platforms provide enough free tools for you to try out their solution, and most webcast distribution partners offer a variety of platform solutions. In general the best approach is to offer a couple of platform options, to cover the widest possible audience if needed and if budgets permit.

Conclusion

Webcasting is a specialized application of streaming media technology. Webcasting systems are comprised of three basic elements: encoders, servers, and players. Webcasting is highly dependent on bandwidth, which determines how much data can be sent in real time from the encoders to the servers, and the servers to the audience. Finally, planning is essential to a successful webcast.

The next chapter covers the basics of digital audio and video. Understanding digital audio and video will help you understand the limitations of webcasting technology, and thereby help you produce higher quality webcasts.

CHAPTER 3

Digital Audio and Video Basics

Webcasting, the latest in a long series of broadcast technologies, became possible due to two parallel developments. First, the tail end of the 20th century saw the rapid development and deployment of digital audio and video technology in the consumer market, in the guise of compact discs, video cameras, and DVD players. This provided the necessary technology that would be adapted to suit the low bandwidth environment of the Internet.

Second, the personal computer, combined with the explosive growth of the Internet, provided the distribution platform. Webcasting combines the power of a multimedia-enabled PC with the interactive nature of the Internet to extend the concept of broadcasting into new territory.

To understand the technical side of webcasting, it is helpful to understand the elements that combine to make webcasting possible, and that begins with digital audio and video. This chapter covers:

- Digital Audio and Video
- Digitizing Audio and Video
- Codecs

Digital Audio and Video

Broadcasting was until relatively recently an analog medium. It wasn't until the advent of satellite transmission that a standard was developed for broadcasting digital audio and video, though the technology had been around for many years.

Digital audio and video offer a number of advantages over traditional analog signals. First and foremost, they are more efficient to distribute. Digital signals take up less bandwidth, because they are encoded more efficiently than analog. This allows broadcasters to use satellite transponders more efficiently, which is crucial because satellite transponder time is very expensive.

This driving force to develop more efficient ways to distribute audio and video signals is the same force behind webcasting, where bandwidth is also an issue. Understanding the challenges of digitizing audio and video will help you plan effectively and educate the crew about the limitations of the medium. To begin, let's take a look at how audio is digitized.

Digital Audio

Figure 3-1 illustrates an idealized representation of an audio waveform. The waveform is a measure of the voltage of the signal over time. This changing voltage is what makes the speaker vibrate, which creates the sound.

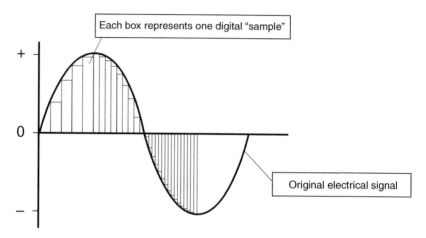

Figure 3-1
An idealized representation of an audio waveform.

To convert this waveform to a digital format, we can measure the voltage at specific intervals, then store these values sequentially. To play back this digital audio file, these values are retrieved and converted back into voltages.

If you look closely at **Figure 3-1** you'll notice that the measured values under the waveform create a stair-stepped representation of the waveform. This is always the case with a digital audio file—it's never an *exact* copy of the original. It's a representation, however close it may be. The fidelity of this representation depends on the *sampling rate* and the *bit depth* of the file.

Sampling Rates — The sampling rate is the number of times an analog waveform is measured, or *sampled*, during a given time period. If you look at **Figure 3-1** you'll see that the first section of the wave has four boxes under it, representing four samples that were taken of the analog waveform. The result is a very rough approximation of the original.

The next section of the waveform has eight samples under it, the next sixteen. As the number of samples increases, the stair-steps get smaller, and the digital version more closely resembles the original. Therefore as the sampling rate increases, so does the fidelity of the digital audio file.

Bit Depth — Bit depth is a measure of the accuracy of the samples taken during the digitizing process. To be as accurate as possible, you have to store larger numbers, and larger numbers use more bits.

For example, you could estimate a building to be two blocks away. Or, you could say it was 300 yards away. To be ridiculously accurate, you could measure it and say it was exactly 10,127 inches away. This is a much more accurate measurement, but you now have to store five digits instead of one.

We want to be as accurate as possible, but higher accuracy requires more digits, and consequently more storage. For example, compact disc audio uses a 44,100 Hz sampling rate and 16 bit samples. Knowing this, we can calculate the data rate for compact disc audio:

```
44,100 samples * 16 bits/sample * 2 channels = 1,411,200 bits per second = 1,378 Kbps
```

Digital Video

Video is digitized similarly to audio in that an analog signal is sampled at regular intervals, and each sample stored sequentially. Video generates a lot more data, however, because of the amount of information that has to be stored.

In the US, NTSC (National Television Standards Committee) video signals are broadcast at 30 frames per second. Each of these frames is subdivided into 525 horizontal lines (approximately 480 of which are visible), and each line divided into 720 picture elements, or *pixels*. Each one of these pixels must be sampled, and the value stored.

Author's Tip

Since even broadband speeds are generally estimated to be in the 2–300 Kbps range, raw digital audio files are too large to be sent across the Internet effectively, precisely because of the sample rates and bit depths used. The challenge for streaming media is to reduce the bit rate of audio so that it can be streamed effectively, while retaining as much fidelity as possible.

A quick calculation shows that each frame of video has nearly 380,000 pixels to sample, and 30 frames per second means over eleven million samples a second are required to accurately digitize a video signal. This is a large number even before we decide how many bits we're going to use to sample the video.

Digital Video Encoding Schemes — Digitizing video is trickier than audio, because there is a lot more information contained within a video signal. If you look closely at your television screen you'll see that it is composed of red, green, and blue dots. Each pixel can therefore be thought of as a certain amount of red, blue, and green. Measuring this would give you three numbers to store for each pixel. This is known as *RGB encoding*.

RGB encoding uses eight bits for the red, green, and blue components of each pixel. However, this is not a very efficient approach, because our eyes are more sensitive to some colors than others. It doesn't make sense to store more information than our eyes can perceive.

Not only that, but our eyes don't divide the world into red, green, and blue components. Our eyes divide the visual spectrum into brightness and color. The technical terms for these are *luminance* and *chrominance*. We are far more sensitive to brightness than we are to color.

Bearing this in mind, a more efficient approach is to assign more bits to the brightness component of a video signal, and fewer bits to the color components. This is known as *YUV encoding*. **Table 3-1** shows some of video data rates using different encoding schemes.

Note that the data rates quoted in **Table 3-1** are in Megabytes per second, not bits. Network bandwidth, however, is measured in bits per second, so the values must be multiplied by eight to show the true impact on network delivery.

Encoding a 320 x 240 frame using YUV 4:2:2, the data rate is 4.4 Mbytes per second, or over 35 Megabits per second. This is clearly an enormous amount of information to send across a network, and far out of the range of most Internet connections. We'll see later in the chapter that special software is used to accomplish this, but first let's explore how audio and video are digitized.

Table 3-1
Approximate data rates of different encoding schemes.

Screen size	RGB (24 bits per pixel)	YUV 4:2:2 (16 bits per pixel)	YUV 12 (12 bits per pixel)	YUV 9 (9 bits per pixel)
720 x 486 (ITU* -R 601 Standard)	30 Mbytes/sec	20 Mbytes/sec	15 Mbytes/sec	11.3 Mbytes/sec
640 x 480 (approx. NTSC resolution)	26.4 Mbytes/sec	17.6 Mbytes/sec	13.2 Mbytes/sec	9.9 Mbytes/sec
320 x 240 (quarter frame, often used in webcasting)	6.6 Mbytes/sec	4.4 Mbytes/sec	3.3 Mbytes/sec	2.5 Mbytes/sec

* ITU: The International Telecommunication Union, a standards body

Digitizing Audio and Video

Most webcasts use traditional audio and video production equipment. The high quality audio and video feeds are connected to encoding computers, which must first convert the analog signals into digital signals, and then encode them. The initial conversion from analog to digital is called *digitizing*. This is done by specialized hardware, either on cards installed in a desktop computer, or an external appliance connected via USB (universal serial bus) or FireWire, two high-speed interfaces built into many multimedia computers today.

Sound cards and Capture Cards

Virtually all computers sold today include a sound card, offering inputs and outputs for the recording and playback of audio. Built-in sound cards are generally sufficient for most streaming media applications; however for true broadcast quality a number of professional sound cards are available. These offer much better signal-to-noise performance and offer higher quality connectors.

Video capture cards are used to digitize video. These cards are available at a wide range of price points, with higher quality provided by more expensive cards. Some video capture cards have built-in hardware enabling real-time control of video quality, which can drastically improve the resulting stream. Any video capture card (or even a cheap webcam) is capable of digitizing video for a webcast, but the stream will reflect the quality of the original source.

External Appliances

Until recently, video capture cards and sound cards had to be installed inside a computer because there were no external interfaces that offered sufficient bandwidth to transfer digital audio and video. This changed with the introduction of FireWire and later USB 2.0. Now a number of external appliances are available.

These offer a number of advantages. First, they are portable and can be moved from computer to computer as needed. Second, in case of failure they're very easy to replace. And finally, they offer high quality and professional connectors (see **Figure 3-2**).

Figure 3-2
The MidiMan USB MobilePre audio interface.

FireWire (IEEE 1394)

FireWire, also known as IEEE 1394 or iLink, deserves special mention, because it is also built in to many camcorders. Digital video and audio can be transferred over FireWire with no quality loss. The FireWire standard also enables control of the camera from the computer. This can be extremely handy when digitizing from prerecorded tapes.

One thing to note, however, is that digital video is encoded using the DV codec, and therefore not quite broadcast quality. While not optimal, for most streaming applications the convenience far outweighs the slightly compromised quality. Webcasting directly from a FireWire input also requires a powerful encoding machine because the signal must be decoded before it is re-encoded to a streaming format.

No matter what equipment you choose to digitize the audio and video, you're still going to have to reduce the data rate. This is done using encoding software, and in particular using a codec. Different webcasting platforms use different codecs, each offering slightly different quality. The following section provides a brief overview of codecs, the magic that makes streaming media possible.

Codecs

A codec (a contraction of coder-decoder) is a software program that determines how audio and video data is encoded for transport and decoded for playback. Codecs use sophisticated mathematics to reduce the data rates of audio and video, while retaining as much fidelity as possible.

Earlier in this chapter digital audio was shown to generate a data stream of over a megabit per second; digital video well over 35 megabits per second. A typical dial-up modem is only capable of receiving 34 kbps; broadband connections typically are capable of sustaining 2–300 kbps. Codecs must therefore reduce the data rates *drastically*.

To do this, codecs take a number of approaches, the most important being to discard information deemed unnecessary. This is determined by using perceptual models, which model how we *perceive* audio and video.

For example, even though our ears are capable of hearing from 20 Hz–20,000 Hz, our ears filter out most of what is going on around us. We pay attention to what is most important to us, and the rest is ignored. Similarly, our eyes can pick out a small detail from everything that is visible in front of us.

The human brain processes audio visual information in a very particular way, and knowing something about this enables codecs to be selective about what information is discarded. With audio, loud noises will *mask* quiet noises, making them inaudible. Also, the human ear is very sensitive to certain frequencies. Codecs can therefore safely discard audio information that has been masked, and devote more effort encoding frequencies that the human ear is sensitive to.

For visual information, our eyes are most sensitive to brightness and movement. Video codecs therefore dedicate most of their resources on things that are bright and things that are moving. Understanding this is a key to producing high quality webcasts, because it affects how camera shots are composed and where microphones are placed.

With audio production, the microphones must point directly at the subjects so as not to pick up other noise. The recording environment must be quiet. You can ensure a high quality audio by taking these two simple steps.

> ## Author's Tip
>
> Video codecs are most sensitive to movement; it is crucial to limit any unnecessary motion in your video frame. This is often counter to traditional broadcast production, where movement is considered to add interest. With webcasting, extraneous motion can seriously affect the quality of your stream.

Codec Side Effects

As good as codecs are today, they're not perfect, which is fairly obvious if you've watched any low bit rate webcasts. Poor audio quality can lead to audio that is muffled, or worse, distorted. This is unacceptable, because audio codecs are so good today that even the lowliest audio-only webcasts should have great quality audio.

Video webcasts often display a number of shortcomings. Poorly encoded video will have *artifacts*, or things that weren't there in the original video signal. These are most commonly described as *blocking artifacts*, where square blocks of color appear in the video.

Webcast video may also have a reduced frame rate. If the original video is too complex to encode at a specified bit rate, the encoder will drop frames to reduce the amount of information to be encoded. This is usually described as *jerkiness*.

Each stage of the webcast process offers ways in which artifacts can be reduced. If you're webcasting at very low bit rates, you may not be able to get rid of all the artifacts, but understanding what to avoid and why codecs are prone to artifacts will help you get the best quality possible.

The Limitations of Streaming Media

No matter how careful you are with your production, there are some limits to webcast quality. Depending on the audience you're broadcasting to and the limits of your webcasting infrastructure, you may have to encode your webcast at a low data rate. By definition, this limits the quality of the audio and video because there simply is not enough data to faithfully represent the original. The lower the data rate, the lower the fidelity.

Thankfully streaming technology has advanced to a point where audio quality is acceptable at very low bit rates, and video quality has improved to a point where a broadband connection is enough to provide an acceptable video experience (see **Table 3-2**). As of 2005, over 50% of US households with Internet connectivity access the Internet at broadband speeds, and this percentage continues to rise. Broadband penetration in other countries is even higher.

Table 3-2
Expected streaming media quality at different bit rates.

Bit Rate	Audio Quality	Video Quality
32 Kbps (56K modem)	FM radio quality	Very small screen (160 x 120 or 176 x 132) Acceptable for talking head content.
64 Kbps (ISDN)	Very good quality. CD quality at approximately 96 Kbps, depending on codec used.	Small screen (196 x 144, 240 x 180) Acceptable for talking head content, poor for high-motion content
256 Kbps (typical sustainable broadband speed)	Excellent	Quarter screen (320 x 240)—Good quality for talking head content, acceptable quality for most content except very high motion content such as sports or music videos.
700 Kbps	Excellent	Excellent quality for all content at quarter screen size (320 x 240); Good quality for full screen (640 x 480).
1.5 Mbps (Ethernet, very high speed Internet connections)	Excellent	Excellent full screen quality for almost all content.

Codec technology continues to improve, and we can expect this to continue, but after nearly ten years of rapid development the improvements are becoming more incremental and aesthetic. The larger issue is the overall capacity of the Internet and how people connect to it, which also continues to improve. Even with the limitations we have today, webcasting is a viable medium with tangible returns for a relatively low cost of entry.

Conclusion

Webcasting combines digital audio and video technology with network delivery. Sound cards and video capture cards are used to digitize audio and video signals. Most networks are bandwidth constrained, so the data rates of raw audio and video must be reduced using codecs. These codecs use perceptual models to make intelligent choices about how a webcast should be encoded.

The quality of streaming media can be somewhat compromised due to the low data rates, but thankfully codec quality is improving, and more people are connecting to the Internet at broadband speeds or better. The next chapter discusses the business of streaming, and what you need to consider before you start planning your webcast.

CHAPTER 4

Business Considerations

The first issues to consider when undertaking any webcast are business issues. You can have the best content in the world and produce a flawless webcast, however, if you don't have a way to measure its success, then it's hard to justify the time, effort and expense you put into it. Specifically the questions to ask yourself are:

- Who is the audience for this broadcast?

- What is the purpose of the webcast? Is it satisfying a particular need? Is a webcast the most efficient method of getting the message out to the audience?

- Where is the webcast taking place? Is the location appropriate?

- When is the event? Is there sufficient time to plan adequately?

- Why? Is there really a demand for this webcast? Will this webcast pay for itself either through revenues or by cost savings?

Thinking long and hard about these questions should enable you to put a rough dollar value on the webcast, which needs to be balanced against the projected cost of the event. If there isn't a good answer for all of the above questions, particularly the last one, do yourself a favor and politely decline. You'll save everyone involved a lot of time and effort, and your stress levels will decline significantly.

If, however, you've got good answers for all of the above questions, or are doing a webcast to learn the process involved, you can start assembling what you need to pull off a successful webcast. To help you with this process, this chapter covers the following subjects:

- Does it have to be live?

- Cost considerations

- Return on investment

- Legal considerations

Does It Really Have to Be Live?

While broadcasting content live on the Internet has its advantages, it is also more expensive than simply recording the audio and video and archiving it for later use. Often, the nature of the content warrants a live webcast, such as breaking news, distance learning where interaction with the instructor is required, an investor's relations call, or a special sports or entertainment event. However, if the content is not of a time sensitive nature you may want to reconsider allocating the resources and budget of broadcasting it live and seek other options for recording and playing it back later as a "simulated" live webcast.

In the early days of webcasting many people broadcast everything live because they wanted the excitement that only comes with a once in a lifetime, truly live event. But these days, with webcasting now looked to as a communication tool (be it for consumers or corporations), using the right form of streaming media is more important that ever before. No longer are people broadcasting live just because they can; they do it when it makes business sense and they have a clear and direct need for the content to be live.

It is also important to keep in mind that it is virtually impossible to tell the difference between a truly live webcast and a "simulated" webcast. A simulated webcast is one that is recorded in advance, encoded, and then rebroadcast as if it were a live stream. The audience experiences it as a live broadcast, since they cannot fast-forward or rewind, and the player often displays some sort of indication that the stream is live. This is how many radio stations, for example, stream on the web stream in a "simulated" live environment.

Author's Tip

If you do broadcast live you generally have the ability to archive it for later on-demand viewing, which, as any webcaster will tell you, is where the majority of the traffic really comes from.

Choosing which solution is best for you should be based on your budget, the type of content, and your perception of what your viewers expect and want. Users have always wanted and liked the ability of being able to view content based on their own schedule so always archive the content whenever possible.

Cost Considerations

Clearly, the single most important aspect of any successful webcast is the cost to produce the event. The final cost associated with your time as well as production services and webcast delivery (bandwidth) will determine if you can show a positive return on investment.

When considering what to spend on a webcast, keep in mind that budget determines both the quality and reliability of a webcast. For instance, having a single backup encoder versus having two or three can change your cost drastically. Shooting an event with three cameras creates a more professional looking webcast, but is much more expensive than using a single camera. At some point, unless you have an *unlimited* webcast budget, you have to decide where to spend your money.

For those who have already spent the money to acquire the equipment you need and have your own network to deliver the streams, your initial capital purchase is your cost of entry. But for those who plan to outsource some or all of the different webcast pieces there are some general guidelines you can follow which will help you figure out what will be the most expensive.

Production Costs

For most webcasts, audio and video capture and encoding are the most expensive components. This is because you need equipment and crew to capture and process the audio and video, and computer equipment to encode these feeds. As the complexity of the production and the number of different streams you're encoding increases, so does your cost. For example, a one-camera shoot encoded into a single format and bit rate could be done with two-experienced people: one person operating the camera and one to handle the audio and encoding tasks.

For a webcast requiring a three-camera shoot, you now need three cameramen, video switching gear, a director and other additional audio and video equipment. All of these factors quickly increase the cost of the production. The number of cameras you use in the webcast is probably the single biggest factor affecting your production cost. For most corporate webcasts consisting of a talking head behind a podium, one camera generally is sufficient. For media and entertainment events that have a lot of action, multiple cameras are typically used.

The incremental cost of adding support for multiple bit rates for your webcast is minimal. With the right hardware encoder, you can encode at multiple bit rates in the same format on one machine. If you want to add another format, you'll need another hardware encoder. But for the most part, one encoding technician can operate three to four encoders before you need to add additional personnel.

Bandwidth Costs

When it comes to delivering your content via the Internet, one of the most confusing and asked about components of the webcast is bandwidth. Much confusion still exists today about what type of network you should use, how that network should be built and what type of bandwidth you must be able to sustain. For those not building their own network, none of those questions matter, but it cannot not be understated how big of a role bandwidth plays in a successful webcast.

If there is one flaw in webcasting versus traditional broadcasting it's that each viewer incurs an incremental cost. With radio for instance, the broadcast signal is in the air for anyone to

> ## Author's Tip
>
> Since every webcast has three core elements consisting of audio and video capture, encoding, and delivery it is important to remember that you can't produce a successful webcast and only expect to have a budget for one of the three pieces.

pull down. It is a limited geographical reach, but radio stations don't pay per listener. With webcasting, you must pay for the additional bandwidth you use each time someone tunes into your webcast. However, unlike terrestrial radio, your webcast can be accessed world-wide. There are pros and cons of every broadcast medium out there and many reasons why you should choose one over another.

While the webcasting industry has matured somewhat, the costs associated with webcasting are still not standardized. Webcasting is slowly becoming commoditized, yet any of you who have tried to get quotes for webcasting services know how frustrating the experience can be. One service provider may charge $500 for bandwidth while another provider may charge $3,000 for the exact same request, delivering the exact same service.

ALERT Raw Internet bandwidth has rapidly become commoditized in the past few years. If you are buying bandwidth based on a per megabit sus-tained model, you can expect to pay somewhere between $75 to $35 per megabit from network carriers. Bandwidth pricing is pretty much even across the board; the more you buy, the cheaper it is per megabit.

If you plan to use a content delivery network (CDN) to distribute your streams, the pricing models can vary widely between different providers. Some providers charge a setup fee per webcast, some don't. Some charge you based on an RSVP model, for instance you say you need to be able to support 1,000 simultaneous users, you pay for that bandwidth whether you get 1,000 users or not. Other providers only make you pay for what you use and charge you on a MB delivered model, anywhere from $1.50 GB to $0.50 GB and lower based on volume. These providers usually have a small minimum ($500) to make sure their expenses are covered.

Bandwidth Measurement Basics — How do you know how large your webcast audience will be? How do you calculate the amount of bandwidth you will use? Once you know how streams, bandwidth, and storage are measured, you can figure this out with some simple math.

Webcast streams are measured according to how much information is sent concurrently, measured in bits per second (bps). For ease of use, larger numbers are measured in Kilobits per second (Kbps) and Megabits per second (Mbps). A Kilobit is 1024 bits; a Megabit is 1024 Kilobits, or 1024 x 1024 bits.

However, the total amount of data sent is measured in bytes instead of bits. There are eight bits in a byte. The Kilo- and Mega- prefixes are used to denote larger amounts. However, since these measurements tend to get very large, a third prefix is used: Tera. A Terabyte is 1024 Megabytes. The other thing to know is that a capital "B" is used as an abbreviation for bytes, to differentiate it from bits.

For example, let's assume you're going to have exactly 100 viewers, and they are all going to watch a 300 Kbps (kilobits per second) stream. Let's first calculate what the concurrent bandwidth usage will be:

```
300Kbps * 100 = 30000Kbps

30000kbps / 1024 = 29.3Mbps
```

So to deliver this webcast you need at least 29.3 Mbps of bandwidth. You should always add 20% on top of this for overhead, which means you need about 35 Mbps of bandwidth for your webcast. That's the concurrent or *sustained* bandwidth you need. The next step is to calculate the total amount of data you'll transfer. Assuming your broadcast is one hour long:

```
35Mbps * 60 seconds/minute * 60 minutes/hour = 126000Megabits
```

But remember, bandwidth transferred is measured in bytes, not bits. So we have to divide by eight, and we can also convert to Gigabytes by dividing by 1024:

```
126000Megabits = 15750 Megabytes / 1024 = 15.38 Gigabytes
```

So now when talking to CDNs with different pricing models, you can figure out what the final charge will be. For your webcast, you need approximately 35Megabits of concurrent capacity, and you plan on transferring approximately 16 Gigabytes of data.

Real-World Bandwidth and Throughput Calculations Example — No webcaster ever truly knows in advance exactly how large their audience will be. In known environments, for example an enterprise, a webcaster may know the potential maximum audience size, but they never know exactly how many will show up. Estimating webcasting bandwidth is always a calculated gamble but one you can become better at as you get to know your audience.

Author's Tip

A full-featured bandwidth calculator that does the calculations for you is available for free as a download from *www.danrayburn.com*. And, you may contact the authors at anytime for help at *help@webcastingbook.com*.

ALERT

One thing to bear in mind is that when it comes to large, public events on the web, virtually all of the numbers after an event are inflated. We know, because we have both done webcast after webcast where audience figures given to the client seem to double, triple or even grow ten-fold when the client puts out a press release.

There are many different measurements of webcasts, such as unique viewers, stream requests, successful stream requests, and average viewing time. For the purposes of estimating your total cost, you need to estimate the total audience size, and the average viewing time. The example in the previous section assumed that each viewer would watch the entire webcast. This is rarely the case, except for webcasts of niche content where valuable information is on offer.

No one knows your content better than you, so you have to judge how long you expect people to watch what you have to offer. For a two-hour webcast, the industry measured average viewing time is about 20 minutes. Obviously this can be shorter or longer depending on the type of content and audience, but it can be a very useful estimating tool.

Let's work through an example. A webcaster is doing a two-hour webcast encoded at 300k and each viewer is expected to watch for 30 minutes. The webcaster doesn't know how many users they expect to get but estimate that in the two hours they may get a total of 10,000 requests for the video stream. Notice the word *requests* and not users because one user could watch the stream twice and it would be counted as two requests. You can do the math the long way as per the previous example, or use the figures in **Table 4-1** for some short cuts.

Table 4-1
Handy transfer numbers for estimating webcast throughput.

Connection Speed	MB/minute	MB/Hour
Dial-up (37 Kbps)	0.27	16.26
Broadband (300 Kbps)	2.20	131.84

Looking at the **Table 4-1**, a 300k stream transfers roughly 65 Megabytes in 30 minutes. Multiply that by the 10,000 requests you expect and if your calculations are correct you will have transferred a total of 650,000 MB or 635 GB. If you're paying $1.50 per GB of transfer, your cost for the webcast will be $952.50.

Now that you understand the basics of calculating bandwidth, determining your bandwidth usage will enable you to better measure your return on investment and estimate what distributing your digital media will cost. Keep in mind this is just an example and depending on the deal you have structured with your provider you may pay more or less for delivery depending on the volume of data you are delivering and the level of commitment you are making.

Return on Investment

Whether you spend $1,000 on a webcast or $10,000, no investment is worth the money if you can't judge how successful it was. Having a defined set of parameters that allow you to see your return on investment is essential. For most people, a large portion of their return on investment is based on the metrics delivered after the webcast. These reports vary in detail based on the distribution service provider chosen but will typically tell you how many people watched your broadcast and the average length of time they watched the webcast.

You also should judge the metrics based on the quality of the message delivered. Was it clear, concise and delivered in the format and manner you intended? Also, if you made your viewers pre-register before the event you have the ability to send them a follow-up questionnaire asking for feedback. This is another great way to measure the effectiveness of your webcast.

The purpose of some webcasts is to make money, the purpose of others to save money, and many are intended for marketing and promotions. Before undertaking any webcast, make sure you have a way to measure for yourself and your organization whether the webcasting medium was the proper and effective way to deliver your message and if you did so in the manner and with the results you were expecting.

Legal Considerations

In the land of entertainment webcasting and especially with content such as radio and music, rights and clearances must always be considered. If you don't own or have rights to the content you are webcasting you need to make sure you secure the proper rights and clearances well in advance.

Get the Right Clearances

There are various legal considerations depending on the content and location of the webcast. For example, anyone webcasting music is required by law to pay royalties to various bodies that have been created to collect payment from webcasters. The radio industry in particular has gone through many years of battles trying to negotiate webcast royalty rates in their favor and has taken the brunt of the legal battles.

Inside the Industry

 Because the laws, governing bodies, and rates tend to change frequently, it is best to go to any of the following websites for the most up to date rules for licensing music:

- www.soundexchange.com
- www.kurthanson.com
- www.live365.com

It's not just music that requires clearance; for example a publisher may have rights to an author reading from a published work. Be sure to research rights clearances thoroughly, and ALWAYS have something in writing that grants you permission and states in detail what you can and cannot do with the content, for instance how long you can host archived versions of the webcast, any geographic restrictions, etc.

Location and Union Permissions

Whenever encoding from a remote location, be aware that some venues may charge a "location" fee just for you to be able to webcast from their facility. This fee can range from a few hundred dollars to thousands of dollars depending on the location and scope of the event. In many cases, paying a few hundred dollars to have the venue allow you to use their Internet connection, phones, security and miscellaneous equipment is a bargain. Those who work at venues, especially the large ones, know who to talk to when you need something and usually know how to get things done quickly, especially if you are in a tight spot. Don't try pushing them aside just to save a few hundred dollars—many times working with people on location can mean the difference between success and failure.

Another location concern is union fees. Many large conference centers and theaters have union contracts, and in these situations you have no choice but to pay them. Unfortunately, these fees can add substantially to the budget, and may prohibit you from using certain locations for live webcasting. As an example, a webcast of the Allman Brothers was scheduled to be out of the Beacon Theatre in NYC until we found out that the union fee was $20,000. Once we let the client who hired us know this cost, they decided to do an audio only webcast as the union fee for audio was only $5,000. Bottom line: do your research, meet the venue manager and learn the details about any location.

Streaming and Digital Media Patents

Beginning in 2003, a number of patent holders claimed that streaming media technology infringed upon their patents, and therefore claimed that they were entitled to licensing fees from any and all streaming content. These patent holders are trying to earn money from their patents as streaming and digital media become mainstream.

Companies big and small are being taken to court and the industry is having both wins and losses. Unfortunately, as with any industry that begins to be successful, these lawsuits and legal challenges are only going to increase. At this time there are so many cases under consideration it's hard to go into detail on any of them.

Author's Tip

For the latest up to date info on some of the more mainstream legal battles taking place you can visit *http://www.streamingmedia.com/ patent/*

StreamingMedia.com provides updated information on streaming media patent cases and how this may affect your business. At this website you can find links to the patents, court documents, contact information for patent lawyers and other resources your company may need.

While this should not scare you away from utilizing streaming media technology, you should at least be educated as to what is taking place in the industry so you can plan accordingly and also make your voice heard.

Conclusion

Understanding these business and legal variables is the first step in planning a successful live webcast on the Internet. Remember that no webcast is worth undertaking if you don't have a way to measure its success, and have a clear and detailed business plan that enables you to leverage the technology. No technology is worth anything if it does not move your business forward.

CHAPTER 5

Choosing the Right Partners

With all webcasts, selecting the right production and distribution partners is a big component of how successful your webcast will be. Rarely can one single-handedly produce a webcast. One partner almost always needs to be involved in the process, be it for connectivity, audio/video (A/V) production, physical distribution or online marketing. Webcasting has come a long way from the early days when webcasting services were hard to come by. Today there are many partners whose sole business is to help you be successful.

Choosing the right partner can be very complicated, especially for new webcasters. Your choice is based on the services needed, location of the webcast, and of course the cost of services. This chapter discusses why you might need a partner and the issues you must consider when making your choice. This chapter covers:

- Do It Yourself vs. Outsourcing
- Distribution Partners
- Marketing Partners

Do It Yourself vs. Outsourcing

The main question to consider when deciding if you should produce a webcast yourself or outsource portions of it is simple: Do I have every resource at my disposal, including equipment and expertise, to make sure this webcast will be 100% successful? If the answer is no, then you need partners.

The majority of webcasts have many partners involved. Very few companies today have the resources to produce a webcast from production all the way to distribution. For the average webcaster, production and distribution technology is not their core business. Webcasting is simply a distribution medium leveraged to broadcast content.

This book aims to provide clear and concise details about all the elements that are involved in a webcast from a technical level. Unless you feel you have all the technology and personnel resources required to produce a webcast, not to mention the bandwidth you will need, then you'll need partners to be successful.

Production Partners

The term *production* is widely used in many industries today. In the webcasting industry, production generally refers to the audio and video production, and is the core of a successful webcast.

Depending on the size, location, and complexity of one's webcast, the number of production partners may vary. Production is critical to the success of your webcast, as even the best content in the world will not attract an audience if it is poorly produced. Choose your partners based on this set of parameters: expertise, price and professionalism.

Expertise

Webcasting expertise is important when considering a partner. When evaluating a production partner, find out what other webcasts they have done. Ask to see some on-demand examples and speak to some of their clients. This may sound like common sense yet many webcasts still fail because of poor production. Don't take their word for it; ask to see some examples and judge for yourself.

Many times, you may be forced to work with a partner that has already been chosen. For instance, many webcasts already have a production company who is capturing the event for other purposes. In this case, having an experienced encoding team who knows how to ask for the best type of feeds and knows how to re-mix the feeds for the webcast is crucial.

Webcasting is not as hard or complicated as people make it out to be, but remember that encoding is more than simply digitizing a file.

Pricing

The most common question is: "How much do webcasting services cost?" We like to answer that by asking another question: "What does a new car cost?" The correct answer is: "it depends." There is no way to answer either question unless you have more information, and in the case of a webcast, you need to know the details of the event and what resources are needed.

While the price for any product or service is always a factor, remember it is not the biggest factor. You can pay a lot for a webcast and have it fail or pay little and have it succeed. Success is based on many factors, of which pricing is only one of the components. That being said, here are some standard pricing rates and the factors that determine what these services cost.

To start with, audio and video production can be the most expensive piece of a webcast if you use multiple cameras. If your webcast requires a single camera, with one operator, producing only one feed, the cost is very affordable at about $1,000 a day—which should include the camera and operator. Naturally, this price can change if it is a last minute request, requires travel, or you need a high quality Betacam instead of a good quality digital video (DV) camera.

> **Author's Tip**
>
> In some cases, up to 8–10 encoders could be required to encode an event and have sufficient redundancy built in. When using this many encoders, you also need the ability to split all the A/V feeds to all the encoders. Pricing for on-site encoding is based on location of event, length of event, formats and bit rates needed, volume of gear and number of personnel. It's impossible to give an estimate without these details but again, it can range based on complexity from $1,000 a day to $10,000 depending on your needs.

Events that require multiple cameras also require multiple operators, a technical producer, a director and significantly more equipment. You may also need a broadcast truck onsite and other large and expensive pieces of equipment. We've seen multiple camera shoots cost as little as $2,500 for two cameras and up to $50,000 or more for five or six cameras. It can get expensive quickly. To find the best price, treat it like any other service: get a number of quotes and check references. There are literally thousands of production companies and many to choose from in virtually every city.

Some A/V houses will also provide encoding services in addition to the A/V production. However, most do not see encoding as part of their core business and realize it is not something they are properly set up to do. If you have the ability to do your own encoding, it's a small event and you're only doing one bit rate or audio only, chances are you can handle it yourself. For events that require many different feeds to encode, at many bit rates and in multiple formats, hiring a partner that specializes in this is the smart move.

Bottom line: know as many details of the event as possible before you call around for pricing. It will save you a lot of time and allow the partner to provide you with a realistic quote.

Professionalism

Professionalism in a partner is often overlooked, but very important. We've both had experiences where unexpected developments can endanger a webcast, such as union issues, connectivity lines being cut, power being turned off, equipment going missing etc. In cases such as these, it's important to have a production partner that knows how to deal with and solve these issues.

Author's Tip

An easy way to find out if the production partner has experience is to ask them what some of the most difficult problems they have had at events have been. All experienced webcasters have horror stories of things that went wrong at webcasts that were beyond their control, but can describe how they were able to work through them to produce a successful webcast.

Sometimes people assigned to work with the webcast team get stressed out during the event and can be difficult to deal with. More often than not, they don't know the importance of the webcast. It is times like these that you will be happy that you hired a production company that knows how to deal with these issues and doesn't let them stop the webcast. Choosing a partner that has the professionalism and expertise to know how to deal with the unions, video production company, security, and everyone else involved at the event *cannot* be underestimated.

Distribution Partners

Most people choose a service provider or a content delivery network (CDN) to distribute their webcasts. Any event, large or small, regional or global, requires a network that is properly set up to receive the incoming encoded stream, distribute the stream over the Internet and report back with detailed statistics after the event. In addition, many webcasters look to partners to help promote the event and make users on the Internet aware the event is even taking place. We'll discuss how you can do both of these successfully and give you some contacts for providers of these services (as well as an idea what it should cost) in the following sections.

Physical Distribution

Since the introduction of content delivery networks, the models by which their services are marketed, priced, and delivered have changed faster than any other aspect of this industry. Choosing the right delivery partner is still a difficult task of cutting through the marketing hype, opinions, and confusing product pitches. Outsourcing all or part of the process can leave you with more questions than answers so we intend to show you how easy it should be.

Most distribution partners don't do a good job of explaining their service offerings. Additionally, their pricing structures can be downright confusing. Many service providers seem to think if they keep the technology confusing and make it sound more complicated than it is, then you will be willing to stay uneducated and therefore always trust what they say. What they don't understand, because they are short-sighted, is that the more they educate the customer, by showing the value of the technology and the potential return on investment, the more the client will utilize them.

Once you have decided to engage a content delivery network to distribute your webcast there are some basics to be aware of. For starters, providers have different names for their products and services, but content delivery is pretty much the same from one provider to the next. Where they differ is the geographic reach, the formats they support, and the add-on services they may provide such as PPV or enhanced reporting.

Deciding which partner to pick should be based on knowing what you need and finding the right fit with the right partner. Some distribution partners will talk about how many servers they have, how many countries they are in and how much bandwidth they can sustain. But if you are doing a small, regional webcast, none of that is really applicable to your webcast.

Author's Tip

The biggest myth when it comes to distribution is who offers the best "quality." Many providers talk about how they offer the best delivery quality, yet from a technical perspective there are few ways to judge this objectively. No third-party organization provides unbiased, reliable data comparing providers from a level playing field. Remember that service quality is not always based on one factor, such as network speed, number of servers etcetera, but rather is usually based on a variety of factors, such as ease of use, price, scalability, and customer service.

Picking the right partner should be like shopping for a car. Get multiple quotes and solution pitches so you have a good understanding of the available options. Educate yourself on company backgrounds and their service offerings. Choosing the right delivery partner is pretty easy if you follow these guidelines and keep in mind the following points before signing a contract.

- **Don't Get Into The Format Wars**: Don't get so caught up in the streaming media format in which your content is distributed. That is actually the easiest part of the equation, because the solution can usually be provided by more than one streaming media format. Delivery partners have an excellent understanding of the pros and cons of each streaming media format; they can recommend the best one based on your goals. Additionally, most providers do not charge extra to distribute one type of format over another. Many times, it is economical to be able to deliver your content in multiple formats.

- **It's All About Setting Correct Expectations**: Always go with a delivery partner that takes the time to educate you and listen to your needs. If they are not willing to educate you before you sign a contract, how much do you think they will educate you after they already have you locked into a deal? No matter how good a deal seems, or what you may have heard of the delivery partner, if the delivery partner doesn't educate you, set your expectations properly and follow up on those expectations, they're not the partner for you.

- **Get First-Hand Advice**: The best information about potential delivery partners is going to come from other webcasters who have outsourced their webcasting. Ask what they have liked and disliked about their delivery partner. Most delivery partners will also let you test their services, to get hands-on with their products and tools. Any delivery partner unwilling to let you test the "packaged" services—for those that do not require custom solutions—is not really interested in winning your business.

Pricing And Providers

Now that you have some idea about how to pick the right delivery partner, what do these services cost and what providers exist in the market today?

For starters, remember that getting pricing for any event without knowing the details is nearly impossible. So to make this easier, I'll use a typical webcast as an example. Also, all delivery partners give price discounts based on signing a contract for multiple events and these can be significant.

All events, no matter the pricing model, are generally also based on length of event, time of event, number of formats/bit rates and geographic distribution needed. Some content delivery networks charge one price to deliver the content globally, others charge based on regions. Keep in mind if you need some sort of registration page, PPV solution, authentication or call them on 2 hours notice, the pricing will be completely different.

For events where the RSVP model is used, the customer estimates how many simultaneous users one may get during the event. While this pricing model is popular, most webcasters tend to overestimate the size of their potential audience. You may pay for 1,000 simultaneous users and only get 300, in which case you paid for something you didn't use. The going rate these days from any one of the leading six content delivery networks is about $1,500 for a two hour webcast for 1,000 simultaneous users in one format. Add more hours, additional formats, interactive features like slides and chat and the price will double.

Pricing for the throughput model varies from $3.00 to $1.00 per gigabyte, depending on volume. However, estimating total throughput is slightly complex, because it depends on estimating the size of the audience, as well as the length of time each audience member is expected to stay connected to the webcast. For a detailed example of how to estimate throughput, please see Chapter 4, Business Considerations. Your best bet like everything else we have suggested is to get multiple quotes from multiple providers.

There are many delivery partners who are a good fit for one customer and not a fit for another. Remember that the right provider is based on what you need, when you need it, where you need it and so on; no one provider is ever a fit for every client. That being said, at the time of the writing of this book, there are five providers who handle most of the webcast traffic on the public Internet. In alphabetical order they are:

- **Akamai** (*http://www.akamai.com*)
- **Limelight Networks** (*http://www.limelightnetworks.com*)
- **Mirror Image** (*http://www.mirror-image.com*)
- **SAVVIS** (*http://www.savvis.com*)
- **VitalStream** (*http://www.vitalstream.com*)

There are others who provide the exact same quality of service for the most part but specialize in webcasting services to the consumer or smaller business market such as PlayStream (*http://www.playstream.com*)Other providers specialize in providing webcasting services just to certain vertical markets like the financial industry with such providers as Thomson (*http://www.thomson.com*) or ON24 (*http://www.on24.com*).

The providers we mention are by no means the only ones offering these services and some of them only offer distribution services in certain regions, or only support specific formats. Also, some have joined programs like Microsoft's Windows Media Certification hosting programs that validate their services, while others have not. Again, we suggest you ask the right questions, get competitive quotes and talk to three to four providers before you decide on the right fit. It should be noted that the authors of this book have worked directly for or worked with every provider mentioned here.

Marketing Partners

Partnering with other websites to promote your event can be a great way to drive traffic to your webcast. In some instances you may not have the right to do this because the owners of the content might insist it remain on only one website. Alternatively, you might relish the exclusivity, and not want to syndicate the content out to others.

If you are looking to create some buzz and awareness for your event, some websites will help promote it if you either pay them or include them as a marketing partner. Many times you can do a barter deal whereby you place the logo of the partner on your website and in exchange they promote your event to their viewers. Other times, you may be able to swap banner ads with other sites so that everyone gets some value in promoting what they want.

Most of these deals are done for events that have a big consumer draw, but other events such as business to business (B2B) webcasts also have locations for exposure. If you have the budget, almost any site will promote your event if you pay them.

Contracts

When you've selected your partners don't forget that like any other service, the contract is going to dictate what you get for your money. Make sure the contract spells out in detail what they are responsible for and a timeline of when everything will be done.

Too many times we see contracts that say someone is going to do on-site encoding, in this city, on this day and here is what it will cost. Where is the info about when they arrive and the formats and bit rates they are providing? Who are they working with on-site at the event location? How many people are they bringing and when is their gear expected to arrive? These and many other questions should all be addressed in the quote for any webcast that requires any on-site production. If it does not give granular detail, ask for a scope of work (SOW) for the webcast. While many partners do not offer SOW's because of the time it takes to put it all down on paper, they will provide one if you ask.

ALERT Be certain the contract states what happens if the partner has any problems on-site. How are you compensated? What are you obliged to pay for? How are you credited for the event if it fails? If the event is outside and bad weather cancels the event, what happens? We have seen event organizers who think they don't have to pay the webcast team because of weather. As with any business arrangement, make sure the details are worked out, and in writing.

Conclusion

Planning for a webcast and choosing the right partners can be compared to organizing an event. Start planning as soon as you know the event may happen, start interviewing partners, figure out a budget and know all the details so you can figure out where the potential problem areas are.

Beyond these considerations, you should be aware that a good partner, one who takes the time to understand your needs, should contribute to a successful webcast. Picking the right partners is tricky because the needs of each webcaster vary, and the available solutions change every year as the technology advances. If you continue to educate yourself, ask questions, and set your expectations correctly, the process will be worth the effort.

Pulling off webcasts that require very little resources can be quite simple, but do yourself a favor and hire the professionals when you know the event requires them. It will save you a lot of frustration and in same cases, your job.

CHAPTER 6

Webcast Production Planning

There are two main reasons why production planning makes or breaks a webcast. First, and most obvious, webcasts are live events, so everything has to work. You can't start over if something goes wrong. Good planning prepares you for problems that arise.

Second, unlike other forms of streaming, everything happens at once. Webcasts are produced, encoded, and distributed in real time. This increases the level of complexity, and requires tighter integration and cooperation on the webcast team.

Taking the time to plan a webcast well in advance makes things run more smoothly. You'll be surprised how issues that could kill a webcast are simple to fix when they're brought up at a meeting a month in advance, rather than ten minutes before a webcast begins.

This chapter covers most (but certainly not all) of the issues you should consider when planning a webcast. The issues are discussed in order of importance and the order they should be addressed:

- Location
- Signal Acquisition
- Equipment
- Crew
- Presentation

Location Concerns

The first thing to consider is the location. Is it appropriate for a webcast? You need to consider the same things traditional broadcasters are concerned with, in addition to some webcast-specific issues:

- Is it large enough to accommodate the required equipment and crew?
- Is there sufficient power and ventilation?
- Is it quiet?
- Is there enough natural light or is additional lighting required?
- Are there union issues?
- Is there Internet connectivity on site?
- Alternatively, is there fiber available and/or is there good access for a satellite truck?

Many of these questions can be answered with a few telephone calls; others may require a scouting trip. If you're webcasting from a remote area, a scouting trip is always a good idea, if only to meet the people in charge. It's a lot easier to get things done when you've established a relationship with the people in charge. Also, on-site connectivity testing is highly recommended—it can save you a lot of trouble later on (see "Connectivity Testing" later in this chapter).

Consider the demands the proposed webcast is going to place on the location. Is there enough room for the equipment, the crew, and the audience? Each camera is going to require a safe, isolated space, preferably with a riser so that people can't walk in front of the camera. Audio/visual (A/V) production can require anything from a six-foot table to a size-able chunk of the room. The encoding (if done on-site) can usually be squeezed onto a six or eight foot table (see **Figure 6-1**).

Typically you want to place the encoding station near A/V production, because that minimizes the cabling required. You should also run the encoding stations from on the same power circuit to avoid ground hums. For more on ground hum, see the "Get Rid of Ground Hum" section in Chapter 7.

Running all this equipment places demands upon the building. Most commercial venues are well equipped to handle the extra power and ventilation requirements, but it never hurts to ask the folks in charge. It's also a good idea to ask if extra charges are incurred.

If your webcast is outdoors, you face a unique set of challenges. By definition outdoor locations are not controllable. You don't know what the light will be like on the day of the webcast, and even more troubling, you don't know if the weather is going to cooperate.

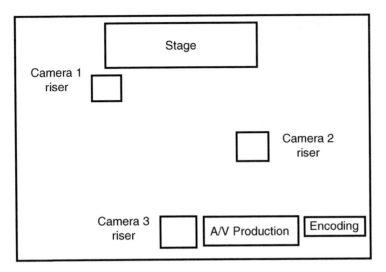

Figure 6-1
A typical setup for a medium sized webcast: 3 cameras (establishment, medium, and close up), A/V production, and encoding.

Make sure you have protected locations for all the equipment. Figure out where power and connectivity are coming from, and how much extra cabling you're going to need. Be sure to hire extra production assistants—you'll need them, whether it's to hold an umbrella over a roaming cameraman, or to buy dry socks for the entire crew.

One of the biggest challenges to outdoor webcasts can be securing some sort of connectivity. If your location is particularly isolated, you may have to get creative, but it's amazing what you can do with a little cajoling and enough time to get things installed.

At the first Tibetan Freedom festival, multiple ISDN lines were bonded together to create the rough equivalent of a T1 line in the middle of Golden Gate Park (which actually caused all payphones in the vicinity to stop working). At the early South By Southwest webcasts, ISDN lines were nailed to trees in the middle of the field behind Stubb's Barbecue. For Bumbershoot, a T1 line was strung through trees from the Seattle Center House to Memorial Stadium, about 500 yards away. In fact, it was re-strung during the middle of the third day when the original cable developed a fault!

Author's Tip

Wireless also provides a fantastic way to get connectivity to otherwise unreachable locations. With the right antennas and unobstructed sightlines you can get connectivity to locations far, far away. As long as you have enough time to plan and test, you can webcast from just about anywhere.

Signal Acquisition

If the location looks suitable, the next thing you have to figure out is how you're going to get the signal to your streaming media servers. There are two basic methods of doing this:

- Send raw media feeds back to the broadcast operations center (BOC) via satellite or fiber channel, and encode at the BOC
- Encode on site, and send encoded streams back to the BOC via IP (Internet protocol)

Sending raw feeds back to the BOC can be advantageous because it minimizes the amount of computer hardware needed on site. However, to do so requires a satellite uplink or fiber connectivity on-site. Both of these options have a high degree of reliability but can be cost-prohibitive. To encode on site, you'll need enough computer hardware and connectivity on site to send the streams to the servers reliably.

Figuring out which method you're going to use is important because it determines what kind of equipment and manpower you need on site. Arranging for either one is time consuming if it isn't already available. For example, you need a minimum of six weeks to get connectivity installed, and that may be too aggressive in some areas. Satellite time and crew must also be booked in advance, though they can usually be turned around in a couple of weeks and even quicker if you are willing to pay a "rush" charge.

Of course, in an ideal world, you'd have both satellite and dedicated IP connectivity at your disposal, but this falls outside the budgetary constraints of most webcasts. Most webcasts today are encoded on site and sent back to the BOC via the Internet.

Dedicated vs. Shared Connectivity

Sending encoded streams back to the BOC via the public Internet is something that has only been possible the past few years. It is never ideal, because the Internet is a shared resource, and bandwidth is never guaranteed. In the perfect world you should have dedicated bandwidth from your encoders all the way to the servers.

For many years this was the way webcasts were done. ISDN circuits and frame relay connectivity offer dedicated, point to point connectivity, which is ideal for a webcast. But both ISDN and frame relay are expensive, often requiring an extended time commitment. The near ubiquitous availability and low cost of DSL lines has led to their rapid adoption for webcasting.

DSL lines come in many varieties, generally specified as a pair of numbers that refer to the maximum download and upload bandwidths. For example, a 1.5/768 DSL line offers a potential 1.5 megabits of download and 768 kilobits upload bandwidth. For a webcast, the upload bandwidth is crucial, particularly if you're sending out more than one stream.

The Importance of Connectivity Testing

There is no way to be sure that the connectivity a location is offering is what they say it is without testing. The connectivity needs of a webcast are far greater than what most providers are used to. For example, most connectivity at hotels and conference centers is shared amongst a number of users. This is fine for web surfers who are checking email, but completely unsatisfactory for a webcast.

Case in point: A small professional organization hired a webcasting provider (read: one of your authors) to broadcast a discussion panel being held in a small hotel conference center. The hotel claimed dedicated T-1 connectivity, which would be more than adequate for the webcast. The organization wanted to keep costs to a minimum, and declined to have the connectivity tested in advance.

When the broadcast began, audience members complained about video quality. Testing revealed that the live streams were dropping frames and stuttering. To remedy the situation, the bit rate of the stream had to be dropped from 300 Kbps to 150 Kbps. This involved stopping and re-starting the encoders, interrupting the webcast, and further aggravating the online audience.

It turned out that the T-1 connectivity at the hotel was not dedicated, but shared by the entire hotel and conference center. When a significant number of users went online, the bandwidth was drastically reduced, leaving insufficient bandwidth to send the higher bit rate streams to the server.

The audience members were livid (they had paid to access the broadcast). The professional organization wanted a refund, but was chagrinned when shown the clause in the webcast contract *specifically* indemnifying the webcast provider against all responsibility—if connectivity testing was waived.

Luckily, an archive was made of the webcast, and distributed to the audience. However, it was barely enough to satisfy the clients. A lot of pain and stress could have been avoided if the connectivity had been tested.

Equipment

There's one simple rule when it comes to equipment for a webcast—redundancy is key. If a camera stops working, another camera must be available to replace it. Similarly, every critical piece of equipment must have a backup in case of failure.

Look closely the next time you're watching the news. On the newscaster's lapel, you'll see a small black clip with not one, but two lavaliere mics. They're not there for decoration.

If you stop to think about what this means, you'll quickly realize that your equipment requirements just increased dramatically. Suffice it to say that you need redundancy in the following key areas:

- **Microphones**: Bring at least one spare mic for the talent, and a spare for the audience.
- **Cables**: Bring lots of extra cables, not only for replacements, but also for that last minute addition to the panel.
- **Cameras**: It's usually too expensive to bring more than a single extra, but make sure you have *at least* one.
- **Audio/Video Mixers**: The backups may not be as fancy as the main mixers, but it's always good to have a spare.
- **Distribution Amps**: You must ensure you can split the media feeds to all the encoding machines.
- **Isolating Transformers and Video Humbuckers**: It's absolutely crucial to have in your kit bag, for solving those unsolvable noise problems.
- **Batteries**: For wireless mics, flashlights, etc.
- **Encoding Computers**: Take at least one, but better to have two or three, depending on how many streams you're encoding.

Author's Tip

Some shipping companies are better than others, so be sure the company you hire is familiar with moving A/V equipment. You may have to pay a premium, but this far outweighs the potential damage. One shipping company we have had particular success with is Rock-It Cargo (*www.rockitcargo.com*).

The amount of spare equipment you bring to a webcast will be dependent on your budget. This is a perfect example of why hiring third-party production for larger webcasts is a great idea. Professional production houses have trucks that include all the equipment you need for a webcast, with plenty of redundancy built in. Remember, they do this for a living.

The final consideration for equipment is shipping. Shipping is the main causes of equipment failure. Production equipment is delicate and generally transported in large, heavy flight cases, but nothing can insulate equipment from aggressive baggage handling.

The Crew

Webcasts require larger crews than other streaming media productions. This is because everything is happening at once, as mentioned earlier in this chapter. Each task must have a crew member attached to it. It's also a good idea to have a few extra crew members available, budget permitting, in case of emergency. At a minimum, you're going to need:

- **Camera Operators**: One for each camera, perhaps more if you're shooting long days and you need to give people lunch breaks.

- **Audio Engineer**: To set up and monitor all the audio equipment.

- **Video Engineer**: Ditto, but for the video equipment.

- **Technical Director**: The guy who calls the shots for the camera operators, and pushes the buttons on the video mixer.

- **Encoding Technician**: The person in charge of all the encoding equipment.

- **Production Assistants**: Also known as gophers, because they're always being told to "Go for" something or other. The more the merrier!

- **Executive Producer**: The person often speaking on two cell phones simultaneously that coordinates the event. This may be you.

You can add or subtract from this list as appropriate for your webcast. For instance you may be hiring third party production, in which case you may only need to provide an encoding technician. Beware of false economies, however—you might *think* that you won't need a production assistant, until something goes wrong. At that point, $250/day is a bargain.

Communication

If you've got a crew with more than a few members, it's important that you have a way to communicate. The director needs to communicate with the cameramen. The encoding technician will need to talk to the audio and video engineers, and with the BOC. On smaller webcasts, it might be possible to lean over and whisper in someone's ear. For larger webcasts, make sure to set up lines of communication.

Professional A/V houses rent out communication ("Com") kits, which enable directors to communicate with the camera operators. These can be expanded to include other crew members. For external communications, cell phones are usually okay, but be sure to test cell phone reception on the scouting visit. Some venues are notorious for having bad reception. In this case, you may need to have a POTS line (plain old telephone system) installed.

> **Author's Tip**
>
> Another way of keeping in touch if you have Internet connectivity is instant messaging. In particular, copying and pasting complicated URLs into an instant messaging window is far simpler than trying to read them over the phone, particularly in loud venues.

Presentation

One thing that should be considered well in advance of the webcast is what the presentation is actually going to look like, and what the experience for the end user is going to be. It's all fine and good to plan on webcasting an event, but what happens before and after the show begins? People tend to arrive early and stay after webcasts are over, so you should take advantage of this and plan accordingly.

The Pre- and Post-Show

If you've ever attended a live television broadcast, you'll recall that before the actual event there's generally a warm-up act. After the show is over, someone else usually comes out and thanks the audience, and reminds them to tune in to watch other related programs. There is no reason you shouldn't do the same thing.

People who arrive early to webcasts should be a) thanked and b) told what time the webcast is scheduled to begin. It may seem like a small thing, but a little common courtesy goes a long way. Background music is good, as well as either a wide shot of the event or a static slide with information about the webcast. Essentially you want to let people know they've come to the right place. There's really nothing more unprofessional that a webcast that begins with a black screen and silence.

Use the pre-show time wisely. Before the show begins is a prime time for marketing messages, or reminders about other events. If folks have tuned in, they're there for a reason, and receptive to the message in the first place. Similarly, when a show is over, thank the audience for attending; remind them about other upcoming webcasts. Let them know where they can find more information about the subject, if applicable, or an email address where they can send feedback.

Use Talent

Taking advantage of the pre- and post-show requires that someone actually get on camera or at least a microphone and address the audience. Make no mistake—this is a skill that not everyone possesses. Ideally you should find someone suited to the task and let them become your on air talent. If you find the right person they'll enhance the webcast, and they may even develop a following of their own.

Technical Difficulties

Another way talent can be helpful is during technical difficulties. For example, if a webcast is running late the audience will be a lot happier if someone goes on air and lets them know what is happening. This might seem like a small thing, but one that will distinguish your webcast and make you look more professional. Of course, starting on time should be one of your main goals, and proper planning will make this a lot easier.

Conclusion

Good planning is essential for successful webcasts. If the proposed location is suitable, get on the phone and make sure you can get the required connectivity on site. Think about what the presentation is going to look like, and what resources it is going to require. Once you've got that process rolling, arrange for equipment and crew, and any talent you might want to use during the broadcast. Have lots of pre-production meetings to make sure everyone involved knows what is going on. Keeping everyone on the same page is half the battle.

CHAPTER 7

Webcast Audio Production

Every webcast should have broadcast quality audio. Good quality audio equipment is cheap, basic audio engineering is simple, and streaming audio codecs sound good at low bit rates. There's no excuse for poor quality—period.

Still, to this day, many webcasts have sub-standard audio quality, which ruins the entire production. People will tolerate sub-optimal video quality if the audio is high quality—the reverse is not true.

To avoid this predicament, this chapter covers everything necessary to produce webcast audio to a high standard. Of course, we can't teach you how to be an audio engineer in a single chapter, but if you follow the recommendations in this chapter, your audio should sound great. This chapter covers:

- Audio Engineering Basics
- Audio Equipment
- Webcasting Audio Engineering Techniques

Audio Engineering Basics

Audio engineering is fairly simple. Sound waves are converted into electronic voltages, which can be digitized and stored on a hard drive. **Figure 7-1** illustrates a digitized sound file displayed in an audio editing program.

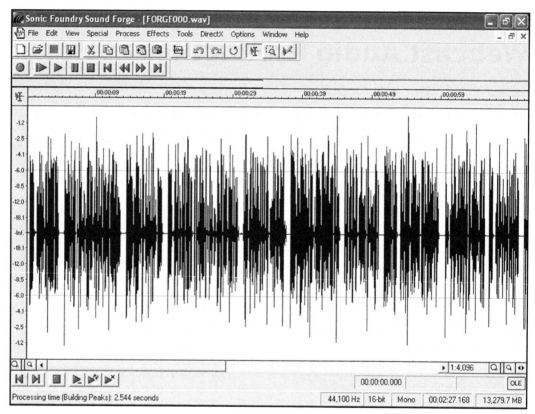

Figure 7-1
A digitized audio file.

At its most basic level audio engineering deals with two things: amplitude and frequency. Amplitude is the measure of the strength or volume of a signal, generically referred to as *level* or *gain*. Frequency is the number of peaks and troughs per second and determines the pitch of the sound. Piccolos generate high frequencies, bass drums generate low frequencies.

As mentioned briefly in Chapter 3, streaming media codecs use perceptual models to convert raw audio into a streaming media format. Codecs use signal level and frequency to determine what is most important about an audio signal, and thereby determine what can be discarded. Knowing a little about how codecs work enables us to produce our audio in such a way as to generate a high quality streaming media file.

Audio engineers strive to record noise-free signals with as much fidelity as possible. Unsurprisingly enough, high quality signals produce the highest quality streaming audio files. Why?

- Broadcast quality audio has a high signal-to-noise ratio, meaning program audio is loud compared to any unwanted noise. A codec therefore sees the noise as "unimportant" or "inaudible" and therefore tends to discard it.
- Broadcast quality audio has high fidelity, meaning a full frequency range and a natural dynamic range. A codec has a better chance of encoding a full-fidelity source file rather than a compromised original.

The first point above is all about level; the second is all about frequency. Our goal, therefore, is to optimize our recording process to get the most level and a full, well-balanced range of frequencies.

Level

Level is the single most important concept to understand in audio engineering, for a number of reasons. First, all equipment has an optimal operating range. At the low end of this range, all audio equipment has internal noise, which is added to any signal that passes through. If the signal is low, the added noise is noticeable. If the signal is high, the added noise will not be audible.

At the high end, audio equipment can only handle signals up to a certain level. If that level is exceeded, distortion occurs. This is audible as a disturbing crackle or buzz. To operate audio equipment optimally you want to use signal levels that are high enough so that no audible noise is being added, but not so loud as to distort.

In addition to internal audio equipment levels, audio engineers must be sensitive to the relative levels of different sound sources in an environment. This is particularly important with streaming media.

Our hearing is incredibly sophisticated. The combination of our ears, as highly sensitive listening devices, and our brains, that adaptively filter this information, enables us to listen selectively. We can pick out a bump in the middle of the night when we're half asleep; we can eavesdrop on the next table in the middle of a crowded, noisy restaurant.

Codecs are nowhere near this sophisticated. Using the noisy restaurant example, the relative signal levels of the hustle and bustle of the restaurant may even exceed the level of the conversation upon which we're eavesdropping. But we can still actively decipher the information that is coming in, and pick out the conversation. Codecs cannot do this. They can divide the audible frequency range into different slices, but cannot distinguish between things that fall into the same frequency range.

Therefore, it is important when producing streaming media to pay close attention to level, both in the equipment (known as the signal chain), and in the environment. The first step is to set up a gain structure for your webcast.

Setting Up a Gain Structure

Gain structure refers to how a signal is being amplified throughout a signal chain. Setting up a gain structure means making sure each and every piece of equipment is operating in its ideal range. To do this, start with the first piece of equipment, and work your way through the chain, checking the levels at each step.

Most audio equipment allows you to adjust both the input and output gain. Most audio equipment also provides some sort of meter to provide a visual indication of the level. **Figure 7-2** shows some examples of audio meters.

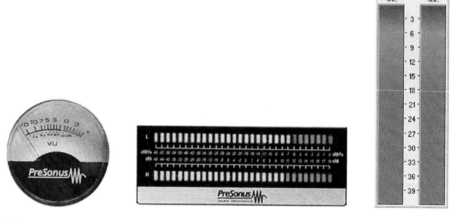

Figure 7-2
Different kinds of audio level meters. Photographs provided courtesy of PreSonus Audio Electronics.

As a simple example, let's take the case of a microphone plugged into a small mixer, which is then plugged into a sound card (see **Figure 7-3**). Starting at the mic and moving towards the sound card, the first thing to be set is the input level of the microphone.

Figure 7-3
A simple audio signal chain. Photographs provided courtesy of Shure Incorporated, LOUD Technologies, and Echo Digital Audio Corporation.

Plug the microphone into the first channel. At the top of the channel strip, most mixers have a knob marked "gain." This adjusts the input gain for whatever is plugged into the channel. They are generally rotary knobs that start at the 7 o'clock position and rotate up to the 5 o'clock position, 5 o'clock being maximum gain. Start with this knob in the 1 o'clock position, which is roughly two thirds of maximum gain.

At the bottom of the channel strip will be a knob or a fader (a square knob that slides up and down) to adjust the level of this channel with respect to the other channels. Start with this at the 0 db (or "U" for unit gain) position. You also must set the master fader for the mixer at the 0 dB (or "U") position.

Speak into the microphone and check the level on the mixer's meters. Make sure you're speaking at a normal level, and at the same distance that it will be when it is being used. Adjust the gain knob at the top of the channel until your level on the meters is in the −6 to 0 db range. Occasional peaks above 0 db are allowed. If you plan on using multiple mics or additional inputs, set the levels for each input in the same manner.

The last step required is to adjust the input level to the sound card. One important note is that input levels for digital equipment must never exceed 0 db.

Inside the Industry

Analog vs. Digital Levels

There is one key difference between analog and digital equipment, and it has to do with how audio signals are measured, digitized, and stored. A full discussion would be incredibly tedious, as there are different methods and scales used to measure audio. This is an extremely simplified explanation.

Essentially, 0 dB is considered to be the maximum signal level, though analog audio equipment can operate at levels significantly higher. This additional range is known as *headroom*. The amount of headroom varies among different types of equipment. Suffice it to say that occasional peaks above 0 dB are fine on analog equipment.

However, 0 dB is an absolute maximum in the digital realm. Because of the way digital audio is stored, there is nothing above 0 dB. If an input signal exceeds 0 dB, the top of the waveform gets clipped off, and the result is known as square-wave distortion. Needless to say, it sounds horrible.

When setting levels in the digital realm, be far more conservative, with peaks in the −10 dB to −6 dB range. This leaves you plenty of headroom for unseen spikes in your audio signal, and keeps your signal distortion-free.

Adjusting the input level for your sound card input can be done in a number of ways. If you're using a standard sound card, open the windows volume control by clicking on the speaker icon in your task bar or selecting "Sounds and Audio Devices" from your control panel. This opens up the Volume Control window (see **Figure 7-4**).

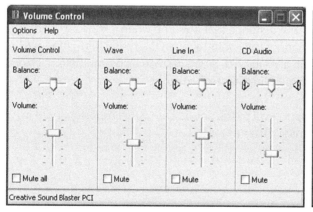 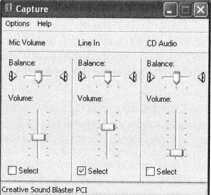

Figure 7-4
The Windows Volume Control windows.

To adjust the input level, select Properties from the Options menu, and select the Recording radio button. This displays software faders for all your input options. You should be using the line input—microphone inputs on sound cards should not be used except in extreme cases, as they're very low quality inputs.

Sound cards have optimal operating ranges just like every other piece of audio equipment. The fader for your line input should be somewhere between 1/2 and 2/3 of maximum. Check your input levels on the application you're using. If you can't achieve a satisfactory level with the software fader, adjust the output of your mixer until your level looks right.

ALERT It's best to set your input levels using the meters included with an audio editing program. The meters on encoding applications are notoriously inaccurate.

Some sound cards include their own mixer. It may look slightly different than the Windows mixer, but the functionality should be the same. Professional sound cards do not allow you to adjust the input level—they assume the input will be at a standard broadcast level. In this case, the input level should exactly match the output level of your mixer. If not, adjust the output level of the mixer until input level to your sound card is appropriate.

Once the gain structure is set, you've ensured that all the equipment is operating optimally, and the minimum amount of noise is being added to your signal. This simple step goes a long way towards ensuring high quality audio.

The best part about setting up a gain structure is that you only have to do it once. You can safely assume that people will always speak into microphones at approximately the same level, and that the relative balance between your inputs will remain roughly the same. You may need to make slight adjustments, but that can be done using the faders on your mixer. In fact, that's exactly what your mixer is for, and why they're indispensable. The next section talks about the importance of equipment and how it can improve your audio quality.

Audio Equipment

Thanks in part to the explosion in home recording, audio equipment is relatively inexpensive. Where once high quality equipment was only available in recording studios, a broadcast quality audio setup can be put together for as little as $500. The equipment you'll need depends on the scale of your webcast, but chances are you'll need a few microphones, a mixing desk (also known as a mixer), a compressor, and some cables to connect it all together.

Microphones

A good microphone is very important because it is the first item in your signal chain. A mic with poor frequency response and dynamics will provide an inferior signal. No audio equipment on the planet can take a bad signal and make it sound good. Microphones come in a variety of shapes and sizes, each with a specific application in mind.

All mics fall into two basic categories, dynamic or condenser. Dynamic mics are rugged and resistant to handling noise, which makes them a perfect choice for webcasts. Condenser mics are more sensitive, have better frequency response, but are highly susceptible to handling noise. Condenser mics are excellent in controlled situations such as studio webcasts.

The next thing to consider when choosing a microphone is the directional response. Some mics are omnidirectional, meaning they pick up sound from all directions. Others, generally known as *cardioid mics*, are more sensitive to sound coming from one direction. For most webcast applications, choose a directional mic, and make sure it's pointed directly at the talent.

Author's Tip

When using lavaliere mics, it's best to use omnidirectional mics. Because they're physically attached to the talent, they don't pick up too much extraneous noise. However, the omni pickup pattern helps when the talent turns their head from side to side.

Finally, there are different types of mics for different applications. Handheld mics can be held by the talent, or placed in a microphone stand and pointed at the talent. Lavaliere, or clip-on mics are clipped on to an item of the talent's clothing, such as a lapel or shirt (see **Figure 7-5**).

It's always best to have a mixture of mics available at your disposal. Some people are comfortable with handheld mics, others are hopeless. You also should consider investing in a wireless mic setup, as it reduces cable clutter and allows the talent far greater freedom of movement.

Shure SM58®
(directional handheld mic)

Audio Technica AT803b
(omnidirectional lavaliere mic)

Figure 7-5
Common webcast microphones a) handheld (Shure SM58) and b) lavaliere (Audio-Technica AT803b). These photographs were provided courtesy of Shure Incorporated and Audio-Technica.

Mixing Desk

Mixing desks (or mixers) are important for two main reasons. First, if you have multiple sources, you need to be able to combine the signals and adjust the relative levels of each. Second, they have high quality mic inputs.

Microphone signals require enormous amounts of amplification. Poor quality mic inputs, such as those available on most sound cards, add noise during the amplification process. Using a mixing desk will get you far better sound quality, so be sure to plug your microphones into a mixer.

Another reason mixers are helpful is that they generally offer equalization (EQ) controls. Later in the chapter we'll see that EQ can be used to improve your audio quality.

Mixers are available in a variety of sizes and price points. Buy one that suits your budget and has enough inputs and outputs for your webcast.

Signal Processing Equipment

There are a number of ways you can process your audio signal to improve the overall quality. These methods are discussed in the next section. These techniques can be achieved using an audio editing program or external hardware. During a webcast, signal processing must be done externally, because encoding requires all the computing resources.

Author's Tip

Some specialized encoding solutions include audio signal processing. These solutions do not require external hardware—but then again, having a backup never hurts.

The two most common types of signal processing are compression and equalization (EQ). EQ will generally be built-in to your mixer, but for specialized applications you may want to invest in an EQ unit. Compression, as we'll see in the next section, is a very useful tool to have at your disposal. You'll almost certainly want to buy an external compressor (see **Figure 7-6**).

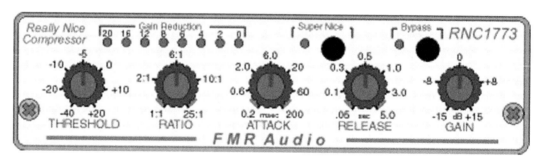

Figure 7-6
FMR Audio's RNC (Really Nice Compressor) 1773. This photograph was provided courtesy of FMR Audio.

Monitoring

It's hard to produce high quality audio if you can't hear what you're working with. If you're working in a studio environment, invest in a good pair of studio monitors. You should have a cheap pair of PC speakers to test your audio quality, but do not use these for critical monitoring. If you're working on location, buy a good set of headphones.

Additional Audio Tools

There are a number of other things that you'll want to include in your webcasting kit. The most obvious is cables. Make sure you've got plenty of cables to connect all your gear together, and bring plenty of spares. Cables are constantly being handled and stepped on, and endure a lot of abuse. However, they do fail, so bring spares.

An assortment of adapters can save your life. While it's always best to avoid using adapters (because they're prime candidates for failure), you may not always have that luxury. You'll probably want to purchase an assortment of microphone stands and pop shields. Pop shields are designed to protect microphones from distortion when people say words starting with the letter 'p.' They come in a variety of sizes and shapes, and are generally seen as foam coverings on the end of handheld mics.

Webcast Audio Engineering Techniques

Once you've set up your equipment and set up your gain structure, you're more or less ready to start encoding. However there are a number of techniques that can make your webcast sound more professional. All of the techniques discussed below fall under the category of "good engineering practice."

Get Rid of Ground Hum

One of the most common problems encountered in location audio production is ground hum. Ground hum is immediately recognizable as a low frequency humming noise in your audio signal. Essentially it is small amounts of the wall power "leaking" into the signal chain. Since wall power oscillates at 60 Hz (50 Hz in Europe and Japan), it is well within our range of hearing. There are two basic steps you can take to avoid ground hums, and a technique to use if all else fails.

1. **Plug all your equipment into the same power source**. If everything is using the same power source, in theory they all have the same ground potential, and therefore no current will leak.

2. **Use balanced cables**. Long cable runs can pick up hum from nearby power cables. Balanced cables employ a simple trick (phase inversion) to improve their noise resistance. Using balanced cables should virtually eliminate this kind of hum.

3. **If all else fails, you can use an isolation transformer**. Isolation transformers connect two pieces of audio equipment without a physical connection. If this sounds like magic, in a way it is—ask any audio engineer at the end of his rope trying to get rid of a ground hum.

Insert the isolation transformer into the signal chain with the proper cables. In webcasting applications ground hum generally appears between the A/V production and the encoding stations.

Ambient Microphones

If you're webcasting a musical event, ambient mics are a must. One of the most important aspects of a live broadcast is the ambience of a live event. Our ears can determine the size of an event by the sound of the audience. If you can't hear the audience, your event will sound flat.

If you're broadcasting from a smaller venue where loud music is being played, there's another reason why you need ambient mics. In this case, much of the music may not be coming through the PA system. If you're getting a feed from the soundman, you'll hear mostly vocals. This is because all the other instruments on stage are already loud enough, or only need a small amount in the PA. Without ambient mics, the mix will sound strange.

It's best to use a pair of ambient mics to get a full stereo effect. They should be placed coincident (in the same spot), in a "v" shape, at 90 degrees to each other, with the microphone capsules (where you speak into the mic) as close to each other as possible.

Deciding how much ambience to use in your mix is an aesthetic judgment and largely dependent on the sound of the room. If the room sound is good, then you can use a lot of ambience. In fact you may want to base the mix on the ambient mics, and then mix in a bit of the PA feed to give the mix some clarity. If the room sound isn't that great, it will probably make more sense to base the mix on the PA feed, and mix in a bit of ambience to enliven the mix.

Author's Tip

If you're in a small venue and trying to capture what is coming off stage, the mics should be about twenty feet in front of the stage, facing the stage. If you're at a large venue and trying to capture the audience, they should be placed at the lip of the stage, facing the audience.

Compression

Compression is an audio engineering technique where the dynamic range of an audio signal is reduced. It can be very helpful, particularly during webcasts, because it makes the audio level more consistent. Consistent audio level is good because there is less chance of a stray spike in the audio level causing distortion. Also, a consistent audio level sounds far more professional.

Television and radio use compression liberally. In fact that's one of the reasons to use compression—people are accustomed to hearing compressed audio. Another good reason to use compression is that it tends to boost the low frequencies, thereby making the audio sound warmer and fuller.

Audio compressors operate by attenuating the audio when it exceeds a certain threshold. Because the loud sections of the signal are attenuated, the overall gain of the signal should be boosted to maintain the original gain structure. This is what creates the consistency and fullness of sound.

Setting up a compressor is easy. **Figure 7-6** shows the front panel of a compressor. Working from left to right, there are knobs to set the threshold, ratio, attack and release times, and overall gain:

- **Threshold**: Determines where the compression kicks in
- **Ratio**: Determines how much to attenuate the signal, with higher ratios meaning more compression
- **Attack and Release Times**: Determine how quickly the attenuation is performed when a signal exceeds the threshold
- **Gain**: Used to restore the gain lost during the compression stage

Start with a mild compression setting. Use a threshold of –10 dB, a ratio of 4:1, an attack time of around 10 milliseconds and a release time of a half second. Send signal through your compressor, and watch the gain reduction meters on your compressor to see how much the signal is being attenuated. Set the gain to compensate for this.

Compare your audio signal before and after compression (most compressors have a bypass switch for exactly this purpose). You should hear a fuller, more "present" sound. Compression tends to bring things forward in the mix, making them sound like they're right in front of you. The more compression you add, the more noticeable the effect becomes.

ALERT Speech is very compression-tolerant. It can be tempting to heavily compress spoken word content, but be careful. A little bit of compression goes a long way. You should always use light to medium compression to keep your levels under control and to make your presentation sound more professional. Add too much, however, and you'll give your audience a headache.

It can be tempting to heavily compress your audio, because of the presence it adds and the increased warmth. Add too much, however, and the programming becomes fatiguing. Take drive-time radio, for example. The DJs scream and yell, the traffic report cuts in, advertisements blare, and each-and-every-word-is-as-loud-as-possible. Sure, it gets your attention, but after awhile it drives you nuts.

Another example is television advertisements. They sound like they're recorded louder than regular television programming, but in fact they're not—they're heavily compressed, which makes them seem extra loud.

Programming should have dynamics. Whether it's a distance learning course or a music broadcast, the natural flow will include some loud and some soft sections. Using compression judiciously reduces the dynamic range, making it easier to control. Using too much compression eliminates the dynamic range, which sounds unnatural, and, as we've all experienced, annoying.

EQ

Equalization, or EQ, is turning up or down certain frequencies in your audio signal. It can be additive, such as adding some low frequencies to "warm up" a sound, or corrective, such as removing harshness from your audio. Either way, the basic idea is to grab a knob and twist until it sounds better.

Most mixing desks come with built in EQ, generally at fixed-frequencies. Because the frequencies are fixed, they are somewhat limited, but can be great to add "just a touch" of EQ. For example, this type of EQ enables you to brighten up a sound by adding a little bit of treble, or warm up a signal by adding a little bass. Similarly, you can get rid of hiss by "rolling off" some high end, and clear things up by turning down the bass.

Author's Tip

If you want to do more surgical EQ, you'll have to buy an external EQ unit, such as a graphic or parametric equalizer. Both these offer much finer control over not only the frequency, but also how much of the frequencies around the target frequency you're adjusting.

To EQ your audio signal, listen closely to your audio signal and ask yourself two questions. First, is anything missing? Does the signal need any low end to warm it up, or some high end for some "sparkle"? If it's hard to understand, it may need a midrange boost.

Next, is there anything that sounds wrong? For example, a muffled signal can be cleared up by turning down the low frequencies. Harsh audio can be tamed by turning down the midrange. **Table 7-1** lists some useful frequencies and descriptions of what they sound like. You can use this table as a guide when using EQ.

Table 7-1
Useful EQ frequencies.

EQ Range	Contents
20–60 Hz	Extreme low bass. Most speakers cannot reproduce this.
60–250 Hz	The audible low-end. Files with the right amount of low end sound warm, files without enough sound thin.
250 Hz–2 kHz	The low-midrange. Files with too much in the low-mids are hard to listen to and sound telephone-like.
2 kHz–4 kHz	The high-midrange. Where most speech information resides. In fact, cutting here in the music and boosting around 3 kHz in your narration makes it more intelligible.
4 kHz–6 kHz	The presence range. Provides clarity in both voice and musical instruments. Boosting 5 kHz can make your music or voiceover (not both!) seem closer to the listener.
6 kHz–20 kHz	The very high frequencies. Boosting here adds "air" but can also cause sibilance problems

Much like compression, it can be tempting to use too much EQ. In most cases you should use mild EQ settings to enhance your audio. If you're twisting any knobs fully clockwise or counter-clockwise, you've gone too far. Be sure to compare your audio with EQ to the original. If there is too much bass or too much treble, you should be able to hear it.

Conclusion

With a little investment in decent audio equipment, and enough time to set up a proper gain structure, you're most of the way towards creating high quality audio, and therefore broadcast quality streaming media. To get that extra bit of quality, use light compression and a bit of EQ to make your audio truly shine.

The next chapter delves into the wonderful world of video, and some techniques you can employ to make your streams look better.

CHAPTER 8

Webcast Video Production

Recent advances in video codec technology have radically improved the quality of streaming video. Additionally, the majority of the Internet audience can now receive high bit rate streams due to the rapid adoption of broadband. The combination of these two issues has made high quality video webcasts a reality.

However, producing a high quality video webcast is still challenging, and begins with producing high quality video. Streaming media encoders must drastically reduce the data rate of raw video. Producing your video to a high standard will make your streams higher quality.

This chapter should give you a firm grasp of the basics of video production, and help you understand how video codecs determine what to encode. This will help you avoid simple mistakes that compromise webcast quality, and enable you to discuss your video production needs with a production company, should you decide to outsource the video production. This chapter covers:

- Video Engineering Basics
- Video Equipment
- Webcast Video Techniques

Video Engineering Basics

To understand video engineering, you have to understand light. When video engineers talk about light, they talk in terms of *luminance* (the brightness) and *chrominance* (the color content of the signal). Producing video, therefore, is manipulating luminance and chrominance. We can add more light, and manipulate the color of the light we're working with.

Just as we saw in audio engineering, video engineers strive to produce a high quality video signal, with plenty of light, color, and as little noise as possible (video noise is visible as excessive grain or "snow" in the signal). High quality video signals produce higher quality streaming video:

- Video codecs use color and brightness to determine what is important in a video signal. Properly produced video provides the codec with better information to encode.

- Video codecs use motion to determine what is important. Video noise is seen as motion, and therefore considered important, and severely compromises your streaming video quality.

Our quest for high quality video begins with lighting, and continues with equipment and video engineering practice. The techniques in this section are standard operating procedure in a traditional broadcast. Later in the chapter we'll discuss techniques particular to webcasting because of the unique limitations imposed by the medium.

Lighting

High quality video requires a lot of light. If you've ever been to a television studio, you'll have noticed that the sets are very brightly lit. Even though many cameras advertise their low-light capabilities, the video they produce under low-light conditions is extremely noisy, which seriously degrades the streaming video quality.

Video shot with insufficient light looks flat and lifeless. Poorly lit video also doesn't encode well, because the video codecs have trouble determining what is important in the frame. Using lights, you can highlight the most important elements and make them "pop" out of the screen. This helps video codecs determine what is most important in the frame, and where to concentrate encoding efforts.

Well-lit video has more vibrant color. Colorful video is more interesting and pleasing to the eye. Video codecs use color to determine what is important in the frame, so producing vibrant video improves your video stream quality.

Lighting for video is half science, half art. Understanding the physics involved is somewhat helpful when lighting a scene, but an experienced lighting designer will also call upon years of experience. A full discussion of lighting techniques is well beyond the scope of this book. However, a brief overview of the most basic lighting setup is provided as a starting point. This technique is known as 3-point lighting.

3-Point Lighting — The simplest of all lighting setups is known as 3-point lighting, as it requires only three lights: a key light, a fill light, and a back light. It's fairly easy to understand, because each added light follows logically. To begin with, we start with a light in front of the subject, which is known as the key light (see **Figure 8-1**).

Figure 8-1
Three-point lighting: a) key light only; b) key and fill lights; c) key, fill, and backlight.

The key light is slightly off to one side of the camera. You can see in the first photo that the subject is lit, but the key light leaves fairly hard shadows across the subject's face. Shadows are important because they create visual interest, but we don't want them too pronounced.

To remedy this, we add a fill light, which is designed to "fill in" the shadows, and light the other side of the subject. Fill lights are generally lower wattage than the key light. In the second photo, we see that the shadows have been softened considerably, and the other side of the subject is now more visible. For a more dramatic shot, reduce the amount of fill light, and leave the shadows more pronounced.

The last thing to do is to separate the subject from the background. This is done by adding a backlight. The backlight should be behind and above the subject, and light the top of the subject's head and shoulder. You can see in the third photo above that the subject now "pops" out of the scene, and is more visually appealing.

Proper lighting provides better encoding quality. The video quality is higher, because cameras produce higher quality images when there's more light. The increased amount of detail and color provide the video codec with more information, indicating what is most important in the frame. Also, by separating the subject from the background, the codec has an easier time separating unimportant content from important content, and focuses encoding resources on what is important.

There are many other lighting techniques that can be used, and many other ways of lighting depending on the situation, but in general you'll find that they're variations on the 3-point lighting technique. If you're producing a large scale webcast, hire a lighting consultant or a lighting company. They'll have the equipment and experience necessary to provide your webcast with appropriate lighting.

Author's Tip

Be sure to tell your lighting crew to light for broadcast. They know that video cameras require additional light, and will light accordingly.

White Balancing

The previous section was all about getting enough light on your subject, or the luminance component of the video signal. We also need to consider the color content, or chrominance component, of our video signal. Once again, it's instructive to consider how our eyes work, and consequently how video codecs work.

Our eyes are extremely sensitive to color. However, we interpret color information differently depending on the total amount of light. For example, a white shirt looks white to us no matter where we see it. However, the quality of light that is reflected off this shirt is entirely different under different lighting conditions. Our brain adjusts automatically, so that colors look consistent to us.

Video cameras aren't as sophisticated. They need to be set up so that a white shirt looks white depending on the available light. This process is known as white balancing, and is very important for professional video productions. Luckily, white balancing a camera is a simple process.

To white balance a camera, have someone hold a white card where the subject will be filmed. Zoom in until the white card fills the entire video frame. Press the white balance button on your camera, and you're done. This indicates to the camera what the color white looks like under the existing lighting conditions. From there, the camera can adjust the lighting spectrum accordingly.

ALERT Many video cameras have automatic white balancing circuitry built-in. These automatic settings are improving, but they're never as accurate as manually white balancing your camera.

White balancing is very important if you're using more than one camera, and if you're shooting in multiple locations. You absolutely must white balance your cameras to keep your colors consistent from shot to shot. If you're shooting an outdoor event, it's important to recalibrate the white balance as the quality of light changes throughout the day.

Warm Cards — White balancing your cameras ensures that all your cameras register colors the same way, by providing them with a standard for white. As described previously, this is done by pointing the cameras at a piece of white cardboard. However, using "warm cards," you can make your video productions look warmer by fooling your cameras into registering colors slightly differently.

Using traditional white balance cards can sometimes result in video that looks a bit clinical. *Warm cards* have a slight tint to them, and therefore skew the color balance of video cameras ever so slightly. The tint is calculated to skew the color reproduction so that flesh tones look warmer. Just be sure to use the same warm card to white balance all your cameras.

Warm cards are available at any good camera and/or video supply store. They are made by a number of manufacturers, and come in a variety of styles and sizes. There are also other cards available that you can use for white balancing to compensate in other ways. For example, if you're shooting in an office with fluorescent lights, you can use fluorescent warm cards to get rid of the green tint that those lights add. You can also use cool cards to get a stylized hard, flat look common in many commercials.

Lighting your subjects properly and white balancing your cameras is the first step towards producing high-quality video signals. Of course, the quality of the signal is going to be dependent on the equipment that you use. The following section discusses the video equipment you need to produce a webcast.

Video Equipment

Though nowhere near as cheap as audio equipment, good quality video equipment is now within reach of even the most modest webcast budgets. The amount of equipment you should purchase depends on the scale (and budget) of your webcast. At a minimum, you're going to need a camera and tripod. Additional lighting, although not strictly necessary, is highly recommended, and will increase the quality of your webcast.

For all but the simplest of webcasts, you're also going to need a video switcher, a monitor, and plenty of cables. A good argument can be made to hire a video production company to produce video webcasts. Production companies usually have package deals that include all the equipment necessary for a broadcast, with plenty of redundant equipment. Unless you plan on producing a large number of webcasts and can justify the cost, hire a production company.

Author's Tip

See Chapter 5, Choosing the Right Partners, for a full discussion of working with partners on your webcast.

Camera and Tripod

A good quality camera is essential. It is the first piece of equipment in your video signal chain, and therefore is one of the main determinants of video quality. Any imperfections in the original signal compromise streaming media quality.

Cameras range in cost from $250 for a cheap consumer grade camera up to many tens of thousands of dollars. Higher priced cameras have far better lenses, higher quality circuitry, and more features. Some features such as digital zoom and in-camera effects are marketing hype and not useful for webcasts. Spend your money on the picture quality, which is the only thing that matters.

Inside the Industry

 Digital video cameras use *charge-coupled devices* (CCDs) to convert the incoming visual information to an electronic or digital format. The quality of the image is determined by the size and number of CCDs used. Cheaper cameras use a single CCD; higher quality cameras use three. CCDs range in size from a sixth to two-thirds of an inch. You should purchase a three CCD camera, with the largest CCDs you can afford.

When purchasing a camera, be sure that it has the outputs you require. Most digital video cameras are now sold with a FireWire output. The FireWire output is perfect for capturing video, but not necessarily the best for encoding live video. To encode a live FireWire source, the video signal must first be decoded to an intermediate format, and then re-encoded to a streaming format. Transcoding requires a lot of computing resources, and therefore a high-powered encoding machine.

ALERT Some video capture cards do not include FireWire inputs and even those that do may not support live encoding. Also, if you plan on using a video mixer, only a handful support FireWire at this point.

It's a good idea to purchase a camera that includes an analog output, ideally S-Video, in addition to a FireWire output.

There are many good resources on the Internet detailing the latest advances in camcorder technology. The main camera manufacturers come out with new models regularly, but there are really only a handful of cameras that are considered workhorses in the webcasting industry (see **Figure 8-2**). If you plan on webcasting regularly, plan on spending at least $2,500 on a good quality camera.

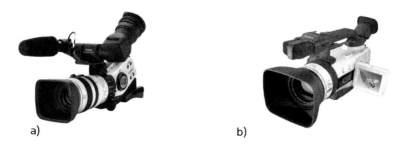

a)   b)

Figure 8-2
Webcast workhorses: a) Canon® XL2®; b) Canon GL2®. Canon, XL2, and GL2 are registered trademarks of Canon Inc. All rights reserved. Used by permission.

Be sure to budget for a high quality tripod. Video codecs use motion in the frame to determine what to encode. Even the slightest amount of motion can degrade image quality significantly. A professional tripod will provide a stable, level platform for your camera. Plan on spending about a third of what you spent on your camera on a tripod.

Lights and Lighting Accessories

To control the quality of your video signal, you must be able to control the light. If you're shooting outdoors, this can be very difficult, because you can't predict the weather, nor can you control the clouds. Indoors, you generally have more control over the lighting, but traditional light isn't designed for video shoots. To manipulate light, you really need professional light sources.

Lights come in many different shapes in sizes, depending on the application. It's best to have a variety of lights at your disposal so you can deal with different lighting situations. Most lighting manufacturers sell kits that include a variety of lights.

If you have the luxury of building out a studio specifically for your webcasts, bring in a lighting consultant. Lights use a lot of power and generate a lot of heat. A professional consultant will sit down with you and determine the extent of your lighting needs, and match those to your studio space.

To complete your lighting equipment needs, you'll need an assortment of gels to color the light, diffusion to make lights softer, as well as *flags* and *barn doors*. Barn doors fit on the front of lights and enable you to control where the light shines. Flags hang from stands and are used to prevent light from spilling where it is not wanted. Some lighting kits include a variety of extra lighting tools. If not, plan on buying extra stands and flags.

Video Switching and Distribution

Video switchers (or mixers) offer multiple video inputs and enable you to switch between them (see **Figure 8-3**). Many also offer cross fading from one source to the next, mixing two sources together using picture-in-picture technology, and titling. Video switchers usually include multiple outputs so you can send the master video feed to multiple encoders, or to an encoder and a video recorder.

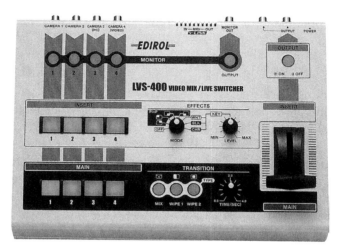

Figure 8-3
The Edirol LVS-400 video switcher. Photograph provided courtesy of Roland USA.

When selecting a switcher, be sure it supports the number and type of inputs you require. For example, most switchers include composite and S-Video (Y/C) inputs, but only a few are supporting IEEE 1394 (FireWire) inputs and outputs. Depending on the number of outputs the switcher offers, you may also need to buy a separate video distribution amp (D/A). Video D/As take a single input and split it into multiple outputs.

Monitoring

Obviously, monitoring your video feed(s) is essential. If you're running multiple cameras, you need a monitor for each camera feed. These can be smaller; often you'll see rack mounted units with three black and white monitors for this purpose. You'll also need a large color monitor to check the quality of the master video feed. The monitors built in to video cameras are for basic reference only—they are not high-quality enough for quality control.

Additional Video Equipment

Finally, there are plenty of other things that are useful for video production that you'll accumulate over the years. Obviously you'll need enough cabling to interconnect all your equipment, and plenty of spares. Buy high quality video cables, because cheap cables are noisy and will affect your video quality. Adapters should be avoided but can come in handy. You'll probably want an assortment of bounce cards, which are used to reflect light, an assortment of cards for white balancing (see "Warm Cards" section earlier in this chapter), and of course a clipboard so you can look official as you run around.

Another handy piece of equipment is known as a *humbucker*. Video cabling is sensitive to ground hums just as audio cabling is. But because ground hum is in the audible spectrum and not visible, it manifests itself as noise or "smear." Humbuckers are inserted into the video chain, and rid the signal of hum much as isolating transformers do for audio signals. Every video engineer will have a handful of humbuckers in their tool kit.

After you've assembled your equipment on set, lit the scene, and white balanced your cameras, you're ready to go. It's at this point that webcast production differs slightly from traditional video production. Webcast production is limited by the abilities of video codecs to faithfully encode the content. Knowing a little bit about how vide codecs operate helps you produce a video signal that is easier for video codecs to handle.

Webcast Video Techniques

For the most part, producing video for a webcast is the same as producing any other video broadcast. However, there are certain techniques that can be applied to improve the quality of your webcast. These techniques are based on the knowledge of how video codecs operate.

Video codecs use motion as the main determinant of where to focus their limited resources. The classic example is the talking head video. In this type of situation, the background of the video is changing very little, if at all. A video codec will focus on encoding the subject's facial movements, and not the background.

However, before the codec can focus on a particular part of the video frame, it must encode the entire frame at least once. This is known as a *key frame*. The first frame of an encoded video stream is by definition a key frame. Following a key frame, a codec will then encode a number of *difference frames*, where only things that have changed between the frames are encoded. After a certain time interval, the codec will encode another key frame, and follow that with more difference frames (see **Figure 8-4**).

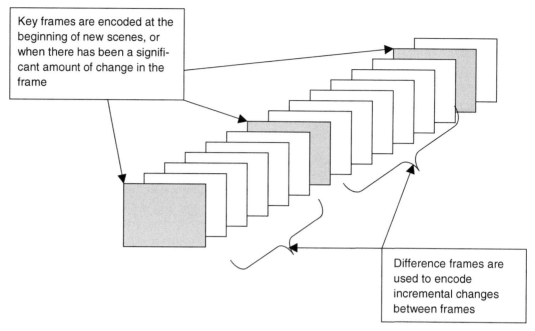

Figure 8-4
A typical encoded video frame sequence.

Key frames require a large amount of data to encode, because every pixel must be encoded. Difference frames, on the other hand, can be economical to encode because only the differences are being encoded. A video codec strikes a balance between key frames and difference frames to keep the average bit rate of the encoded stream constant.

Video codecs must always encode a key frame whenever the amount of change in the frame exceeds a certain threshold. For example, cutting to a new scene or camera angle forces a key frame to be encoded. Video codecs also encode key frames at timely intervals to keep the frame as sharp as possible.

ALERT Problems arise when there is too much motion in the frame. In this case, the video codec is forced to economize in a number of ways. The difference frames must be encoded at lower quality to accommodate all the change in the frame. Additionally, the quality of the key frames may have to be compromised to keep the overall bit rate manageable. This limitation dictates the overarching rule of webcasting video production—keep motion to a minimum.

All the techniques described in the following sections will increase the quality of your webcast video. However, if they're followed to the letter, your webcast runs the risk of being as interesting as watching paint dry. At the end of the day your goal is to get your message across in the most effective way possible. The idea is not to limit the creativity of your webcast, but keep in mind the load you may be placing on the video codec.

Keep Motion to a Minimum

Producing webcast video is somewhat contrary to traditional video production. Most cameramen and editors use motion to add visual interest throughout a video. But as the previous section explained, motion is anathema to video codecs. So producing a successful webcast is often riding the fine line between artistic intention and the limitations of the medium.

Probably the most important thing to do is to use a tripod. Even the most seasoned cameraman is incapable of holding a camera absolutely still. Even the most infinitesimal movements can appear to a video codec as movement, and thereby degrade the video quality significantly.

Another thing to avoid is shots that include movement, such as pans (movement from left to right), tilts (movement up or down), and zooms. While these shots may add interest, they're very difficult for a video codec to deal with. If you need a closer shot, a better approach for streaming video is to have another camera get into location for the shot, and then to switch to that camera. Using this method, the change is drastic but very short; the codec can encode a new key frame, and then return to encoding difference frames.

After switching to a new camera angle, stick with it for awhile. Remember that when you switch to a new camera angle, the video codec will sense a scene change and encode a new key frame. Most video codecs are designed to encode a new key frame every ten seconds or so. Cutting much faster than this will cause your video quality to degrade as the codec struggles to keep up with the cuts.

When switching to new shots, use simple transitions such as quick cross fades or hard cuts. Transitions done with special effects such as "page turns" or explosions are extremely difficult to encode. These transitions also do damage that outlasts the transition.

Consider how a codec treats a complicated transition:

1. When the transition begins, the video codec senses a scene change, and encodes a key frame.

2. After a few difference frames, which are more expensive than most difference frames because of the amount of motion, the video codec decides there is far too much change for mere difference frames, and encodes another key frame.

3. This process repeats throughout the duration of the transition, and the video codec simply runs out of bits. It may take five to ten seconds for the codec to recuperate enough to be able to encode another key frame.

Not only does the transition look bad, but the video immediately following the transition is compromised.

ALERT Quite frankly, the other reason to avoid fancy transitions is that only amateurs use them. Using gimmicky transitions only highlights the fact that it's an unprofessional production, and one that ends up looking horrible on the Internet.

Video Signal Processing

If you're using good quality equipment, have enough light, and are following the simple production techniques described previously, you're most of the way towards creating high quality video streams. However, there are a few things you can do to give your production that extra bit of shine. These are due to the fact that television monitors and computer monitors use different technology, and display things differently.

Television technology is well over 50 years old. They are far less detailed than computer monitors, and we sit much further away from them. Television and computer monitors also process color differently. Consequently, when video shot for television is displayed on a computer monitor, it usually looks a bit dull and washed out. You can use video processing to compensate for this.

Video signal processing can be done using hardware or software, but during a webcast it is generally done using an external video processing amplifier, or *proc amp* (see **Figure 8-5**). Proc amps usually offer knobs to adjust brightness, black levels, saturation, and hue of the video. Brightness and black levels refer to the luminance of the signal; saturation and hue refer to the chrominance.

To make video displayed on a VGA monitor look like it does on a television monitor, you generally need to add a bit of brightness and saturation. Be careful, though, because if you

Figure 8-5
A typical video processing amplifier (proc amp).

add too much brightness, things will look too washed out. Similarly, add a bit of saturation to make your colors more vibrant, but don't go overboard.

One thing to bear in mind is that you should only adjust the video that is intended to be viewed on a computer monitor. If your production will be distributed on DVDs as well as streaming versions, only adjust the signal that is being encoded for streaming versions. If you add extra brightness and saturation, and then view the result on a TV monitor, the video will look too bright and gaudy.

Inside the Industry

 As if things aren't tricky enough, PCs and Macs have different gamma settings. Gamma refers to how the mid tones are reproduced. Basically this means that images and video look different on a Mac. Unless you want to create special versions for your Mac audience, it's just one of those facts of the Internet that you have to live with.

Conclusion

Video production depends on light, and your ability to control it. Consequently be sure to use plenty of light, and a good lighting engineer to help you achieve the look you want. Make sure to white balance all your cameras for consistency, and try experimenting with warm cards to get a warmer look to your video.

Spend enough money to get a good quality camera if you're going to be doing a lot of webcasts, and don't forget to buy a high quality tripod while you're at it. Finally, keep motion to a minimum if you want your encoding quality to be optimal. Of course you're never going to be able to eliminate all motion from your webcasts, but keeping this rule in mind will help you produce video that encodes better.

Now that you know how to produce high quality audio and video, it's time to delve into the world of encoding. Encoding software has improved to the point where it's fairly straightforward to use, but knowing what all the settings do will help you understand how it works.

CHAPTER 9

Webcast Encoding

The encoding stage is where webcasting production separates from traditional broadcasting. Encoding is where the broadcast quality we have worked so hard to produce thus far is compromised. Unfortunately this comes with the territory: there simply is not enough bandwidth available on the Internet to stream broadcast quality video. Yet.

This may not always be the case. There are a number of initiatives in the works to deliver fiber connectivity to the home, which would offer upwards of 30 Megabytes per second downstream capacity. Also, webcasts destined for use on internal networks can take advantage of multicast, and deliver much higher bit rate streams. Regardless of the bit rate you are streaming, you have to use an encoder to convert the raw digital media into a format that can be streamed.

This chapter covers the entire encoding process including a discussion of advanced encoding techniques and explains what equipment and hardware is essential for a successful webcast. Included in the chapter are step-by-step examples of how to encode using Windows Media Encoder and RealProducer software. In order, the topics covered are:

- Encoding Basics
- Encoding Equipment
- Webcast Encoding Techniques
- Encoding Settings Examples

Encoding Basics

At their most basic, encoders take incoming audio and/or video and encode a streaming version according to the parameters you provide. Encoders use sophisticated mathematics and perceptual models to retain as much fidelity as possible. The fidelity of an encoded stream is directly related to the bit rate: the higher the bit rate, the higher the fidelity.

Modern audio and video codecs have improved dramatically in the last decade, and continue to do so. Combined with the increasing penetration of broadband, this has made webcasting a much more enjoyable and high quality experience. But not everyone has a broadband connection, and broadband streams use a lot of bandwidth. Therefore, the first thing you have to do when considering encoding settings is to consider your audience.

Consider Your Audience

When planning for a webcast, take a moment to consider who your target audience is, and what limitations that imposes on your webcast. If you're webcasting on the public Internet, there are a number of things you need to consider. Although many people have broadband connections that are rated at a megabit per second or greater, this data rate isn't sustainable across the public Internet for long periods of time.

The public Internet, as of 2005 and into 2006, is capable of sustaining streams in the 300–500 kbps range. Certainly there are networks capable of sustaining much higher data rates, but all it takes is one outdated router to cause a bottleneck for your entire webcast. Testing in advance can help here.

Another thing to consider is the aggregate bit rate you'll be delivering simultaneously. A single 300 kbps stream isn't much, but webcast to one thousand people simultaneously and you're looking at 300 Mbps, which is considerable. Delivering that amount of data requires a serious streaming media infrastructure.

 ALERT You should also consider the aggregate total bandwidth delivered, as many streaming providers charge by this measure. Using the preceding example, one thousand viewers watching a 300 kbps stream for an hour consume approximately 128 Gigabytes of bandwidth. For most streaming media hosts this isn't a considerable amount of bandwidth. However, if you're being charged per gigabyte, you can tailor your stream bit rate to accommodate your budget.

Consider Your Programming

The other main concern is the type of programming you're encoding. In the preceding chapter we learned that motion is difficult for video codecs. However, no matter how careful you are when producing the program, there is bound to be motion, and in some types of programming much more than others.

Sporting events, for example, are notoriously hard to encode. The nature of most sports is motion, and lots of it. There may be steps you can take in the production stage to minimize the motion, such as framing your shots a bit wider, and cutting to different camera angles less often. However, you still need to consider the programming as a whole, and set your encoding parameters accordingly.

Encoding parameters are discussed a little later on in this chapter, in the "Webcast Encoding Techniques" section. Before we delve into the actual settings, let's take a step back and talk about encoding equipment.

Encoding Equipment

Encoding equipment is simple: a computer with a sound card, video capture card, and encoding software. A modern processor with decent speed is all you need for most applications, though if you're trying to do something fancy such as encoding multiple streams on a single computer, you'll need a high-powered CPU.

Computer Hardware

For most applications you can work with the minimum amount of RAM the operating system requires, though additional RAM never hurts, particularly if you may be running other applications on the same computer at the same time. 512 Megabytes of RAM is probably the minimum you need. Hard drive space is the same—if you're not archiving locally, then you don't particularly need a lot of storage. However, if you're planning on archiving your files locally, be sure to have enough drive space to store your archives (see **Table 9-1**).

Table 9-1
File sizes for different bit rates.

Bit Rate	One Hour File	Hours of Storage per Gigabyte
37 kbps	16 Megabytes	64
128 kbps	56 Megabytes	18
300 kbps	132 Megabytes	7 3/4
700 kbps	308 Megabytes	3 3/4

Bear in mind that you may be webcasting both dial-up and broadband versions of your webcast, and encoding multiple formats. In that case, you could be generating over a gigabyte an hour for your content. However, with 60 GB hard drives available as standard on most computers, storage is rarely a problem.

You need a sound card. Many computers come with sound cards, some of them built-in to the motherboard. Most computers sold today are aimed at consumer grade applications, with sound cards expected to perform mundane tasks such as playing back operating system sound effects. The quality of the components used is not particularly high, and consequently the built-in sound cards tend to be noisy. If you're producing a high quality audio feed, the noise may not be apparent. Using a higher quality sound card or an external audio device is always a safer bet.

To capture your video signal, you'll need a video capture card. Video capture cards come in a range of prices with a multitude of features. Most consumer capture cards today are targeted towards folks who want to watch TV on their computers and may want to record television programs. These cards tend to be lower quality and focused more on the TV tuner than the video quality.

Inside the Industry

 What you're looking for is a video capture card that accepts a composite or S-Video input. Some capture cards include a FireWire input which can be used as both the audio and video source. However, as mentioned earlier in this book, encoding a DV signal requires the encoding computer to first decode the incoming DV signal before it can re-encode it to a streaming format. This is possible, but requires a fair amount of computing horsepower. Check with your software manufacturer for recommended minimum requirements.

Because of the way Windows and Mac operating systems deal with audio and video, you'll most likely need an encoding computer for each stream you plan on offering. In addition, you'll want to have at least one if not two backup encoding machines ready to go for redundancy purposes. The backup machines can also be used to monitor the streams, the servers, and to keep in touch with other people working on the webcast via instant messaging.

Computer Software

The software you need depends on what format you're using for your webcast. At a minimum, you'll need the encoding software offered by the manufacturer, such as the Windows Media Encoder or the RealProducer. Most modern computers are capable of encoding a webcast with plenty of CPU power to spare, though in general it's best not to run other software on your encoding machines.

You should have at least one computer that is dedicated to administrative tasks, such as monitoring the streams locally, monitoring server activity, and possibly running instant messaging software. Obviously you'll need media player and instant messaging software installed. You may also want other software tools, such as stream editors, or audio and video editing software. If you're webcasting a number of events over the course of a few days, you can utilize down time to do some editing for archiving purposes.

Specialized Encoding Equipment

There are a number of encoding solutions available for webcasting. Some are designed to work around the operating system limitations that restrict an encoding machine to a single stream of output. Others are designed to combine streaming media with other assets such as PowerPoint slide presentations to create a unified presentation. Depending on your webcast and budget, one of these might be a worthwhile investment.

Multiple Stream/Format Solutions — There are a number of custom webcasting systems available that enable a single machine to encode multiple streams of output. High powered machines have more than enough horsepower to encode multiple streams, but are limited by the way the operating system handles resources such as sound cards and video cards. These systems work around these limitations to offer multiple streams from a single encoder.

ALERT Multiple stream solutions are a double-edged sword. On one hand, it makes sense to utilize all the computational power that an encoder has to offer. On the other, you now have a single point of failure for a number of streams. If, for example, the network interface on the encoder fails, you don't just lose a single stream—you lose all the streams that are being encoded.

That being said, multiple stream solutions are a great solution, provided you build enough redundancy into your encoding system. They're also great because far less encoding hardware is required on site, which means a smaller footprint for the encoding station.

Inside the Industry

 The following manufacturers offer multiple stream solutions as of Fall 2005:

- Communitek Video (*www.communitekvideo.com*): offers the minicaster and Webcaster encoding stations

- Digital Rapids (*www.digital-rapids.com*): Offers the DRC-Stream™ line of hardware

- Sunnyside Software (*www.sunnysidesoft.com*): Offers Raycaster software which enables multiple streams of Windows Media.

- Viewcast (*www.viewcast.com*): Offers SimulStream software that works with their Osprey series of capture cards, and the Niagara Streaming Systems (see **Figure 9-1**).

- Winnov (*www.xstreamengine.com*): Offers the XstreamEngine line of encoders

Figure 9-1
The Viewcast Niagara Power Stream Pro.

Presentation Solutions — One of the most common webcast formats is talking head video combined with some sort of presentation, such as PowerPoint slides. To produce a webcast of this type requires some fairly advanced authoring and production skills. A number of manufacturers have devised solutions that bundle this functionality into a single interface:

- Accordent (*www.accordent.com*): Offers PresenterPlus, PresenterPro and Pre-senterOne software, as well as the Accordent Capture Station hardware solution.
- Sonic Foundry (*www.sonicfoundry.com*): Offers mediasite™ hardware solutions.
- Webcast in a box (*www.webcastinabox.com*): Offers an all-in-one webcasting appliance (see **Figure 9-2**).

Figure 9-2
The Webcast in a box encoding solution.

Production/Encoding Hybrids — Some encoding solutions combine audio and video production capabilities with encoding. These typically include multiple video and audio inputs, switching capabilities, as well as audio and video processing.

- NewTek (*www.newtek.com*): Offers the TriCaster (see **Figure 9-3**), which bundles video capture, editing, live production, and Windows Media encoding.
- Sony (*www.sony.com*): Offers the Anycast production and encoding system.

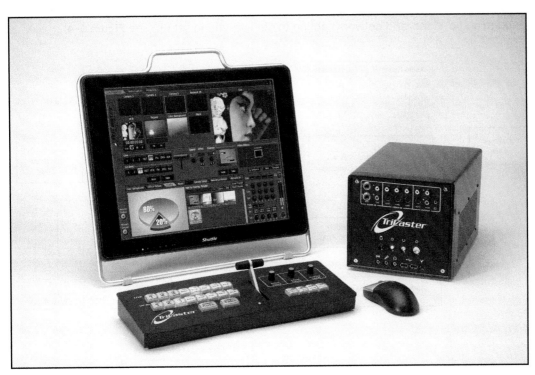

Figure 9-3
NewTek's TriCaster.

Setting Up for Redundancy

The number of encoding machines you require depends on a number of things. First of all, you have to figure out how many different streams you're planning on delivering, and how many streams you're going to encode on each machine (if you're using multiple encoding technologies). On top of that, you need at least one backup machine, preferably two.

For example, if you're encoding Windows Media and Real streams, at broadband and dial-up rates, you'll be encoding four separate streams, requiring four encoding machines. Add in two spares for redundancy, and you're looking at six encoders. Don't forget you'll need enough audio, video, and network cabling to get everything set up (see **Figure 9-4**).

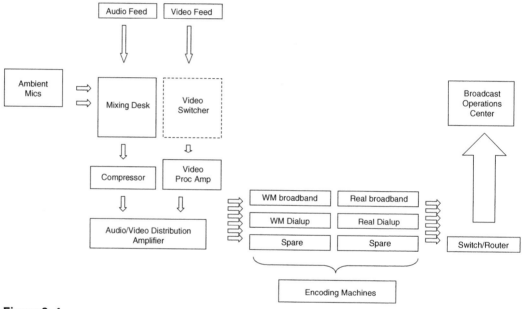

Figure 9-4
A typical redundant encoding setup.

Author's Tip

Most encoding software offers a way to save all the encoding settings to a file. Save settings files for all your streams, on the desktop. That way if an encoder fails, a replacement stream is only a click away.

When you set up your encoding equipment, label each machine according to the format and bit rate of stream it will be encoding. If a stream goes down, you'll know immediately which encoding machine is down, and which cables to check. Another good tip is to copy the encoding settings for all streams to the backup machines.

Webcast Encoding Techniques

Encoding a webcast is no different than encoding any other streaming media file. All the same considerations apply. You have to consider the audience you're trying to reach, and how much bandwidth they have. Your encoding settings follow from this, as with all other streaming media.

Bit Rate Considerations

The majority of all webcasts are now done at broadband bit rates. Some webcasts include a dial-up stream to cater to the widest possible audience, but this will not be the case for much longer. However, even though the audience will be predominantly on broadband connections, it's worth considering what your broadband bit rate should be.

The public Internet is capable of sustaining approximately 300 kbps. This is a fairly safe bit rate to use. However, if you're expecting a huge audience, you may want to scale this back to 200 kbps or even 150 kbps. Even though higher bit rate streams provide higher fidelity, it's of no use if they cannot be delivered. The simple fact is that lower bit rate streams stand a better chance of successful delivery.

You should also consider if there are other aspects of the webcast, for instance slides that will be delivered along with the video. If so, be sure to leave some bandwidth for the other media assets. You also should leave some bandwidth for the audience to use email, chat, instant messaging, and all the other things that people use when they're online.

The other consideration may be budget. If you're paying for your bandwidth, 150 kbps streams cost half as much as 300 kbps streams to deliver. For talking head content, 150 kbps should be sufficient to deliver adequate quality. Experiment with different settings during your testing to determine what your minimum bit rate should be.

Author's Tip

Remember, you can always contact the authors of this book for help on encoding techniques or anything else in the book. Email us at *help@webcastingbook.com*.

Audio Considerations

There are a number of things to consider about your audio, the first being the bit rate. Obviously if it's an audio-only webcast the entire bit rate will be audio. But if you're webcasting video, you have to decide how much of the available bit rate to dedicate to the audio stream.

Table 9-2 lists suggested minimum audio bit rates and the quality you can expect for each. Note that the presets that come with most encoders often use lower audio bit rates, particularly for dial-up streams. This is not necessarily the best approach.

Table 9-2
Suggested minimum streaming audio bit rates and expected quality.

Bit Rate	Minimum Audio Bit Rate	Quality
Dial-up (34–37 kbps)	8 kbps	AM radio
Low Broadband (64–128 kbps)	16 kbps	Nearly FM radio
Standard Broadband (200–300 kbps)	32 kbps	FM radio

In addition to the bit rate, there are two other settings you can control. You can choose to use a voice or a music codec, and you can encode in either mono or stereo. It's easy to decide which to use in both cases.

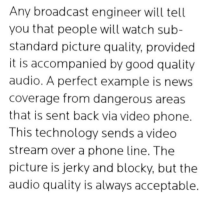

Author's Tip

Any broadcast engineer will tell you that people will watch substandard picture quality, provided it is accompanied by good quality audio. A perfect example is news coverage from dangerous areas that is sent back via video phone. This technology sends a video stream over a phone line. The picture is jerky and blocky, but the audio quality is always acceptable.

Most program content is mono. Even music that is recorded in stereo places the important elements in the center of the mix. At any given bit rate, mono codecs have higher fidelity than stereo codecs. Not only that, but stereo codecs sound pretty bad at bit rates less than 32 kbps. So unless your content truly requires stereo, encode in mono and your content will sound better. You should always encode in mono at bit rates under 32 kbps.

The choice between a voice codec and a music codec is a little trickier. Voice codecs take advantage of the limited frequency and dynamic ranges of speech, and use a different algorithm to encode a higher quality stream. The problem is that if you try to encode music using a voice codec, it sounds horrible.

Video Considerations

The total bit rate of your file constrains the video quality of your webcast. Recall that video codecs must render key frames followed by difference frames, and must stay within the budget that is determined by the total bit rate. Once you decide on a total bit rate for your stream (and the audio codec you're using), there are really only three basic encoding settings you can control: the screen size, or *resolution*, the frame rate, and the *frame quality* setting.

Resolution — Let's start with resolution. If you're webcasting at dial-up rates, you simply are not going to be able to deliver a full-screen, full-motion experience. The crazy thing is that encoding software will let you try. You can set up an encoding profile with a resolution of 640 x 480 and a total bit rate of 34 kbps—but don't expect the result to resemble anything other than mud.

So the thing to do is to choose a resolution that is appropriate to your total bit rate and the type of content you're trying to encode. High motion content will require reduced resolutions to achieve acceptable results. Low motion content will encode well at slightly larger screen resolutions than high motion content. This is yet another area where testing before your event will be very helpful. Determine in advance what resolution is optimal for your bit rates. **Table 9-3** lists some suggested resolutions for different types of content at varying bit rates.

Table 9-3
Suggested screen resolutions.

Bit Rate	Low Motion Programming	High Motion Programming
Dial-up (34 kbps)	176 x 132	160 x 120
Low Broadband (64–128 kbps)	240 x 180	192 x 144
Standard Broadband (200–300 kbps)	320 x 240	240 x 180

One important thing to notice about the suggested screen resolutions is that they're a 4:3 *aspect ratio*. The aspect ratio is the ratio of the width to the height of the picture frame. You should always use a 4:3 aspect ratio when setting the resolution. Aspect ratios and screen resolutions are discussed in more detail later in the chapter in the "Cropping and Resizing" section.

Frame Rate — The second setting you can set is the frame rate. Standard video is shot at 30 frames per second (actually 29.97). Ideally we want our streaming video to encode at 30 frames per second. Unfortunately, when encoding at a low bit rate, there may not be enough bandwidth. One approach is to reduce the frame rate.

However, reducing the frame rate may be a false economy. For example, consider encoding at 15 frames per second instead of 30. To do this the encoder drops half the frames, and encodes every other frame (see **Figure 9-5**). Remember, however, the codec encodes based on the difference between frames. If there is a lot of motion in the programming, the difference between frames 1 and 3 will be greater than frames 1 and 2. So even though there are fewer frames to encode, the difference between frames may be more difficult to encode.

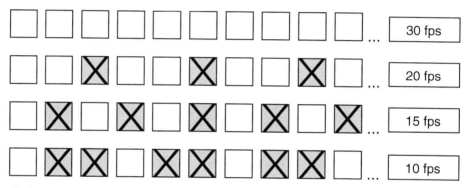

Figure 9-5
How encoders drop frames when encoding at reduced frame rates.

If your programming is low motion, decreasing the frame rate can help, because the difference between frames is minimal. If your programming is high motion, stick with the original frame rate and decrease your resolution until you achieve acceptable results.

When reducing the new frame rate be sure the new frame rate is a factor of the original frame rate. To see why, consider the examples in **Figure 9-5**. To get 15 frames per second, the encoder drops every other frame. For 10 frames, the encoder encodes a frame, then drops two, then encodes one, and drops two, etc. The key here is that the time interval between encoded frames is consistent.

If you specify 20 frames per second, the encoder encodes two, then drops one, encodes two, etc. The problem is that the resulting encoded file will appear jerky, because the difference between the first two frames is a single frame, but the difference between the second and third is two frames. The time interval between frames is inconsistent, and the result will be ugly.

Frame Quality — The final setting you can affect is frame quality. This setting determines the overall quality of the video frames. The encoder uses the frame quality setting and the frame rate to determine how to encode your file. Setting the frame quality high means you'd prefer less frames per second, but higher quality. Setting the frame quality low means you'd prefer the encoder to provide the full frame rate, and compromise picture quality to achieve it.

In the Windows Media and QuickTime encoders, you set a frame quality between 1 and 100, with 100 being the highest frame quality. The RealProducer offers three settings, Sharpest Image, Normal, and Smoothest Motion. High action programming generally looks best when encoded with low quality frames, because the motion requires a full frame rate. Lower motion programming can often take advantage of a higher quality frame quality, and hence a lower frame rate.

Inside the Industry

 Ben Waggoner, noted industry compressionist, feels most viewers prefer a stable frame rate with variable image quality to stable image quality with a variable frame rate. To achieve this, you should set your encoder's frame quality controls to minimum. Of course, the big exception is when image quality is at a premium, for example in a classroom where a whiteboard has to be legible.

He also feels that frame rates below 12fps aren't a good idea. There is greater change between each frame (which needs to be encoded), and the user has more time to notice each artifact.

The solution? Use a lower screen resolution.

The best approach to encoding is to start with an existing encoding profile and to experiment with the settings. If your content is low motion, you can experiment with larger resolutions and higher frame quality. Higher action programming will by definition require reduced resolutions, and lower frame qualities.

Using Advanced Encoding Filters — In addition to the basic settings that you can control in your encoder, most encoding software also offers advanced filters to deal with special situations. Two of these are designed to deal specifically with issues that arise during the video transfer process, the third deals with poorly produced content.

DeInterlacing Filter — The resolution section touched on the fact that television and computer monitors display video differently. Another difference is that television monitors are *interlaced* displays, whereas computer monitors are *progressive* displays. Interlaced displays divide each frame of video into two fields, one that includes all the odd lines and the other all the even lines. Progressive displays don't have fields, they just have a single frame (see **Figure 9-6**).

Interlaced video divides a frame into two fields, sampling (and displaying) the odd lines first, and the even lines second.

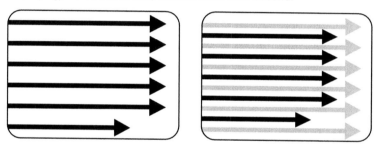

Progressive video does not have fields. A frame of video is sampled and displayed by starting in the top leftcorner and rendering all the lines *progressively*.

Figure 9-6
Interlaced vs. progressive displays.

To make a single frame of progressive video, the two fields of interlaced video must be combined. The problem arises because the fields are actually separated by a discrete interval of time, 1/60th of a second to be exact (1/50th of a second in Europe). If there's a lot of motion in the frame, particularly horizontal motion, the combination of the two fields can cause problems (see **Figure 9-7**).

Figure 9-7
A progressive frame assembled from two interlaced fields.

The vehicle driving past the camera moved considerably between the first and second fields. Consequently, when the fields are combined into a single frame of progressive video, the result is that the vehicle is a mess. Deinterlacing filters attempt to remove interlacing *artifacts* from the video before it is encoded.

There are a number of different ways that interlacing can be mitigated. The details are complex and tedious—suffice it to say that most video content should be deinterlaced for maximum quality, with a couple of notable exceptions.

The first exception is when you're encoding at a resolution of 320 x 240 or smaller. In that case, most encoders don't use the second field, so interlacing artifacts never appear. The second is if you're filming with a new video camera that supports progressive mode, in which case the programming isn't interlaced to begin with.

Inverse Telecine Filter — The inverse telecine filter gets rid of the redundant frames that are created when film is transferred to video. The native frame rate of film is 24 frames per second. When film is transferred to video, an extra frame is inserted every four frames. This frame is "created" by combining fields from the frames surrounding it.

The extra frame isn't noticeable when the video plays back, but it's unnecessary. An inverse telecine filter senses the extra information and removes it, so that the codec doesn't have to waste effort on encoding redundant information.

Noise Filter — The final filter, a noise filter, is useful only for poorly produced content. Low quality content is noisy, which is visible as grain or snow in the picture. This grain is seen as motion by the codec, and thereby seen as important.

A noise filter slightly blurs each video frame, thereby reducing the amount of detail. Reducing the amount of detail in the frame generally reduces the amount of motion seen in the frame, and thereby tricks the codec into ignoring the noise.

If you produce your video content to a high standard, you should never have to use a noise filter. However, for content that can't be re-shot or otherwise fixed, a noise filter can help.

Cropping and Resizing — Virtually all streaming video has to be resized at some point. The limited data rates that we can encode at generally preclude any sort of full screen presentation, so we're generally encoding at something less than 720 x 480. However, there's another reason that streaming video has to be resized, due to the difference between television and computer displays.

Aspect Ratios and Square vs. Non-Square Pixels — Television screens have a 4:3 aspect ratio, which means the ratio of their width to height is always a perfect 4:3. However, television displays have 480 visible lines of resolution, each line having 720 pixels. If you do the math, you'll see that this is not a 4:3 aspect ratio. A 4:3 aspect ratio would dictate 640 pixels per line.

When video is digitized at 720 x 480, and displayed on a computer screen, the image looks a bit squashed because of the difference in pixel geometry. To solve this problem, we have to resize the video to a 4:3 aspect ratio. When we resize a 720 x 480 digital video to a 640 x 480 or 320 x 240 resolution, we're restoring the original aspect ratio that television pixels would otherwise provide.

Why It's Tricky — First of all, resizing, by definition, changes the original signal, and it's a very complex thing to do. If done incorrectly, it can introduce artifacts into your video signal. These artifacts will be amplified by the encoding process, and may result in a low quality video stream.

Cropping the image adds a level of complexity, because you have to be extra careful about maintaining your aspect ratio. Some instances where you might want to crop your video are:

- You're encoding from a very low quality source, which has noise around the edges or along the bottom.

- You're encoding widescreen content that has been "letterboxed" with black bars along the top and bottom of the screen.

These two cases require completely different approaches. In the first case, you want to stay at a standard 4:3 aspect ratio, but get rid of some noise along the edges. In the second case, you want to end up with a 16:9 widescreen aspect ratio (or some variation thereof).

The first thing you must determine is what the final aspect ratio of your video is, and choose a resolution accordingly. If it's a standard 4:3 aspect ratio, then the usual 320 x 240, 240 x 180, 192 x 144, and 160 x 120 are what you should be targeting. If you want to end up with a widescreen format, then you should be targeting a 16:9 aspect ratio, like 320 x 180, 240 x 132, or 160 x 90.

Next, you must determine how much you want to crop your screen, and adjust it to maintain a 4:3 (or 16:9) aspect ratio. If you want to crop 5% of the bottom of your frame to get rid of noise, you're going to have to also crop 5% from either the left or right sides to maintain your aspect ratio (see **Figure 9-8**).

Author's Tip

Many codecs have limitations on the resolutions they will handle, caused by their minimum macro-block size. This is a fancy way of saying that the dimensions may have to be even multiples of 4, 8 or even 16.

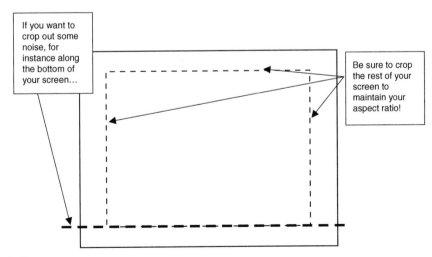

If you want to crop out some noise, for instance along the bottom of your screen…

Be sure to crop the rest of your screen to maintain your aspect ratio!

Figure 9-8
Be sure to maintain your aspect ratio when cropping.

Depending on what software you're using, you have to determine in what order the resizing and cropping are done, so you can maintain the proper aspect ratio. Some of the cropping functionality offered by encoding applications can be downright confusing. Examples of cropping and resizing are provided later in the chapter.

Legacy Considerations

One very annoying consideration that you must bear in mind as a webcast producer is what version media player your audience has installed. This can be particularly relevant in the enterprise, where desktops may be locked down and users are not allowed to install software. Some of the latest codecs in encoding applications are not backwards compatible with older players.

For example, if you're webcasting to a corporate audience that is standardized on a Windows 2000 platform, and they have not upgraded to Windows Media 9 Series, you cannot encode using the Windows Media 9 video codecs. The audio codecs are backwards compatible, but the video codecs are not. This is particularly frustrating because the Windows Media 9 Series video codecs represent a huge step forward in video quality. You may be forced to encode using Windows Media 7 codecs, which offer far less fidelity.

This situation is by no means limited to the Windows Media Platform. Real, QuickTime, and Flash all have the exact same problem. In an ideal world you'd always encode using the latest codecs for the highest possible quality. Depending on your audience, you may be limited to lower quality legacy codecs.

Multiple Bit Rate (MBR) Files

If you're encoding a number of different bit rates and more than one encoding platform, you can quickly end up with a lot of files. Not only that, but instead of a single link to a webcast you may have to put four or more links (i.e., broadband and dial-up bit rates, in both Windows Media and RealMedia formats). To simplify this, both Windows Media and RealNetworks allow multiple streams to be embedded in a single file, known as a multiple bit rate (MBR) file.

MBR files offer a number of advantages. First, they allow you to use a single encoder to encode multiple streams, reducing the amount of equipment you need. Second, file management is simplified, with a single link to the content for all bit rates, and a single archive file to keep track of. Additionally, RealNetworks Helix servers have the ability to switch between streams contained within the same file. This feature is known as SureStream technology. This can be helpful if traffic conditions on the Internet change during a webcast.

The ability to switch to a lower bit rate stream made for a much improved experience for the audience when the technology came out. Connectivity on the Internet has improved a lot in the past five years, however, making this functionality largely unnecessary. While the improved file management is useful, the switching ability largely is not.

Not only that, but the resolution of all video streams in a SureStream file must be the same. This renders it practically useless, because different resolutions are appropriate for different bit rates. With SureStream, you end up either encoding at a small resolution, which is not an optimal experience for the broadband audience, or at a larger resolution, which dooms the dial-up stream to inferior quality.

Push vs. Pull

There are two basic methods used to get your stream to the server:

- **Push encoding**: Using this method the encoder initiates the connection, and sends the stream directly to a server.

- **Pull encoding**: Using this method, the server initiates the connection, requesting the stream from the encoder.

Push encoding can be advantageous because it enables you to encode from behind a firewall. The server doesn't have to know anything about the encoder, however, to set up a push encode you must know the server name, port, and other information such as the publishing point, or a username and password combination. All this must be set up in advance on the server.

Pull encoding can be advantageous because it requires no knowledge on the encoding side. All you have to do is start up the encoder, and the server takes care of the rest. However, pull encoding requires that the encoding machine reside on a *routable* IP address. This means that either the encoding machine cannot be behind a firewall, or if it is, you'll have to do some work on the firewall configuration to make sure the server can request packets from the encoding machine.

The encoding method you choose is highly dependent on how your distribution network is set up. Some content distribution networks (CDNs) only support pull encoding, others require push. It will also be dependent on the network connectivity on site and whether routable IP addresses are available. Be sure to test your encoding well in advance to avoid any surprises right before the broadcast.

Encoding Settings Examples

The techniques described in this chapter are for the most part available in all live streaming applications. The biggest challenge is figuring out where each platform hides the settings, and what the terminology used by each platform means.

The following sections illustrate how to set up encoders for the Windows Media and Real platforms. Both of these encoding applications are available for free, though the RealProducer Basic does not allow you to alter the default templates. It's actually really simple to get around this limitation of the RealProducer. All audience templates are stored in the audiences folder, in a fairly simple to understand XML format. Open any of these files in a text editor, change the settings any way you like, and save the edited file. Presto!

For the purposes of this exercise, we're going to assume that we're catering to a broad-band audience. Depending on your audience you may also want to encode a dial-up stream when you webcast. For Windows Media streams, you can simply choose another encoding template and use a multiple bit rate file. For Real streams it's generally best to encode two separate streams and offer different screen resolutions for each. The following examples should familiarize you with the encoding applications enough to do what you need to do.

Windows Media Encoder

The Quick Start section of this book provided a step by step walk through the Windows Media Encoder using the wizard. Now that you've read most of this book, it's time to start acting like a power user. Start up the Windows Media Encoder. If the New Session Wizard appears, de-select the check box in the lower right corner that says "Show this dialog box at start up," and click cancel (see **Figure 9-9**).

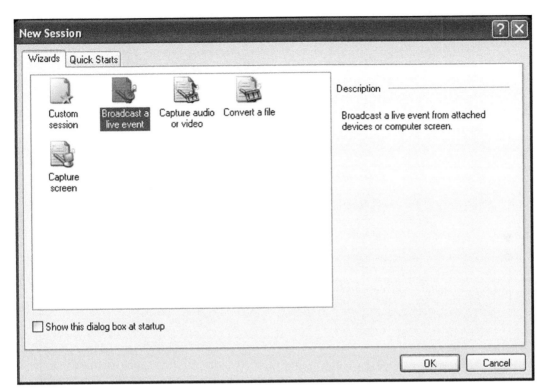

Figure 9-9
Disabling the Windows Media New Session Wizard.

All you have to do now is click the Properties tab along the top of the Windows Media Encoder. This opens up the Session Properties window in the left side of the Windows Media Encoder. The window presents a tabbed interface to all the encoder settings. In fact, when you use the New Session Wizard, you're essentially working your way through these very tabs. The first tab is where you set up your sources for the webcast (see **Figure 9-10**).

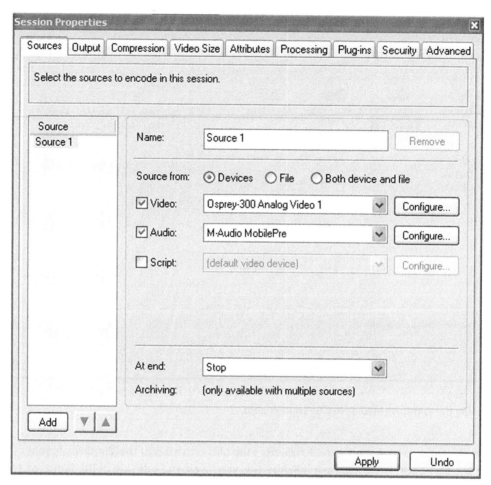

Figure 9-10
The first thing to do is set up sources for your webcast.

Selecting Sources — Choose an audio and a video source for your webcast. In most cases these will be from devices, but in some cases, for example if you're using an intro and outro, you may want to define previously existing files to use. For each file, you'd set up a different *source*.

The Windows Media Encoder is very flexible when it comes to setting up sources. You can define a number of different sources, and define behaviors for each of them. For example, consider a webcast where you want to display a welcome slide for the 30 minutes preceding a broadcast, then webcast a live audio and video feed, and then finish off with a thank you slide for five minutes. In this case you would define three different sources.

The first source would use an image for the video, and perhaps live audio. Source two would be live audio and video, and source three would be another slide for the video, and perhaps with previously recorded audio. During the broadcast you could switch between these sources, manually, or have them switch automatically at certain times. This is an easy way to produce a relatively professional looking broadcast.

After your sources are set, it's time to set up how you're going to send your streams to the outside world. This is set up on the Output tab.

Select Your Output Method — Click on the output tab to set up how you're sending the encoded stream to the server (see **Figure 9-11**).

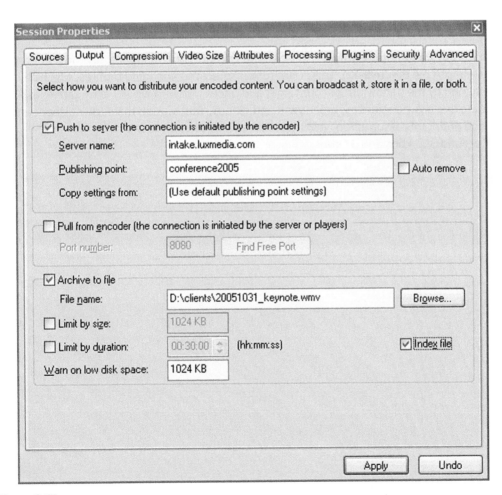

Figure 9-11
Next, set up your output method(s) on the Output tab.

If you're using the push method, click the "Push to server" box, and enter the server name and publishing point. If you're using the pull method, click the "Pull from encoder" box and make sure the port you're using isn't in use by any other applications on the machine. If you need to change to another point, be sure to tell your distribution partner the new port number—they'll need to know that to set up the server correctly.

The last thing you can do on this tab is create an archive of your webcast. You can do this by checking the "Archive to file" box, and providing an appropriate file name. The archive can be limited by size or duration, if you're worried about filling up your hard drive. In these days of 100+ gigabyte drives, this should not be too much of a concern. The next step is the heart of the encoder—the compression tab.

Choose Your Encoding Settings — Click on the Compression tab to display the compression settings (see **Figure 9-12**). This is where you select the encoding profiles, which are determined by the bandwidth of your target audiences. These days, it's fairly safe to assume there are two basic audiences, broadband and dial-up, with dial-up thankfully disappearing. Working under this assumption, you should be aiming to encode two streams, targeting bit rates around 300 kbps and 37 kbps.

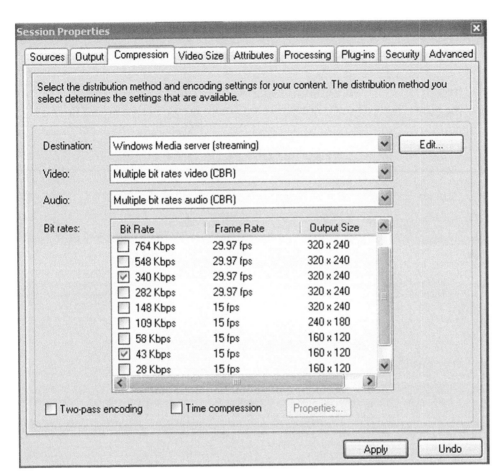

Figure 9-12
The Compression tab is where the fun begins.

The Windows Media Encoder exposes different default profiles depending on which selections you make in the Destination, Video, and Audio drop down menus. Select "Windows Media Server (streaming)," "Multiple bit rates video (CBR)," and "Multiple bit rates audio (CBR)." Then select appropriate bit rates for your audience. To modify an existing profile, click the Edit button to bring up the Custom Encoding Settings window (see **Figure 9-13**).

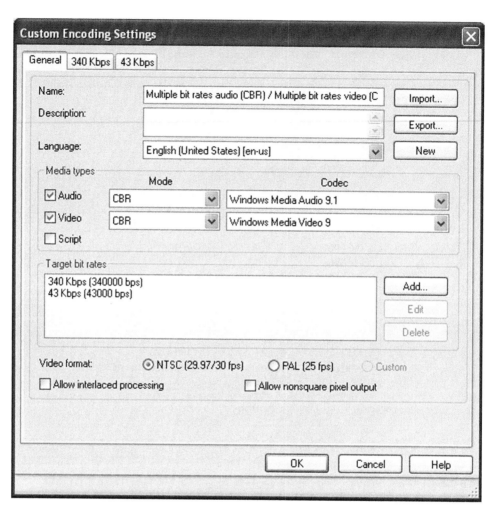

Figure 9-13
Use the Custom Encoding Settings window to optimize your settings.

For example, the default streaming profiles provide a 340 kbps and a 43 kbps. You can modify each of these by clicking on the appropriate tab in this window. You can choose which audio codec to use, adjust the total bit rate by raising or lowering the video bit rate, and adjust the screen resolution. There are other advanced settings you can adjust, such as key frame interval, but you shouldn't really mess with these unless you really know what you're doing. In **Figure 9-14**, you can see that I've created a custom 300 kbps profile, with a 32 Kbps mono audio codec, and the video bit rate adjusted to 259k for a total of 300 kbps.

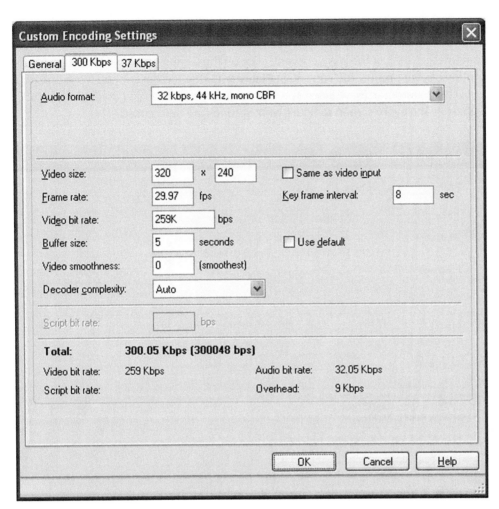

Figure 9-14
A custom 300 kbps profile with a modified audio codec and video bit rate.

If you put a decent amount of effort into creating a custom profile that works for your content, you should save it so that you don't have to re-create it each time. After you have your parameters set just the way you want, click on the General tab, and type a name and a description of your profile. You can see in **Figure 9-15** that the description leaves no doubt as to how the parameters have been set. This saves time later, as you don't have to click through each and every screen to figure what settings are being used.

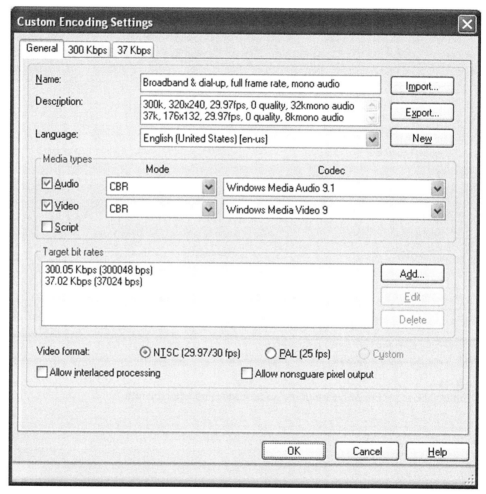

Figure 9-15
Save your custom profiles with sensible names and full descriptions.

Adjust the Video Size — Click on the video size window if you need to do any cropping of your video. But beware—cropping your video is not a trivial exercise. There is significant interplay between the settings on this page and the settings you specified on the Compression tab.

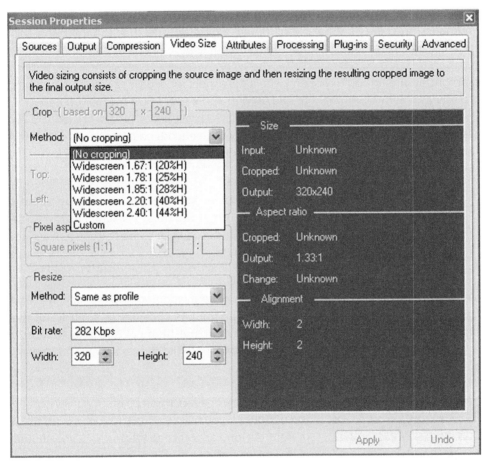

Figure 9-16
Try to avoid resizing your video if at all possible.

The Windows Media Encoder comes with a number of presets for cropping 4:3 content to a widescreen aspect ratio (see **Figure 9-16**). However, by default, Windows Media Encoder attempts to stretch the video to fit whatever resolution you set on the Compression tab. So if you're trying to encode a widescreen aspect ratio, you must be sure to set the output size on the Compression tab appropriately.

For example, if you're cropping letterboxed content for a target 16:9 aspect ratio, you should set your output size to 320 x 180 or any other 16:9 aspect ratio. Then, on the Video Size tab, you should select the 1.78:1 setting (which is the same as 16:9). The result will be a nice widescreen file.

The Windows Media cropping utility is clever in that it uses percentages instead of exact pixel numbers. The benefit is that if your input is a different size than you think, the encoder will crop the same *percentage* of the screen. It might sound tricky, but it works.

For example, assuming you're working with a 4:3 aspect ratio, using a size of 320 x 240. To get to a 16:9 aspect ratio, you want to end up with 320 x 180, which means you have to crop 30 pixels off the top and bottom. Choosing the 1.78:1 preset does precisely that. The cool thing is that if your sources are actually 640 x 480, the encoder automatically changes the settings to crop the right percentage of the screen, so your output looks correct.

ALERT The one drawback to the Windows Media Encoder cropping utility is that it doesn't preview in real time. You must start the encoder to see the results of your settings. Be sure to run some tests to make sure you're getting what you want.

If you're cropping to get rid of noise at the edges of your video, you have to use the custom method of cropping. This is where you can get into trouble, because the controls for the amount of cropping on all four sides are independent. Furthermore, the default behavior of the Windows Media Encoder is to stretch the picture to fit the size specified in the Compression tab.

Author's Tip

You can shave off 5% of all four sides without any problem. This part of the screen is hidden by most television sets by the plastic surround, so cameramen and directors never put anything important at the extreme edge of the picture. For a 320 x 240 screen, this translates to 12 pixels off the top and bottom, and 16 pixels off the left and right.

The key is that for every three pixels you shave off the top or bottom, you have to shave four pixels off the left or right. As long as you keep this in mind, you should be okay. But be careful.

Fill in the Stream Information — Click on the Attributes tab to fill in title, author, copyright, rating and description information (see **Figure 9-17**). This information is optional, but highly recommended. If you don't provide this information, the player defaults to displaying the name of the file in the title bar, which might be totally meaningless. It's much better to display a meaningful title. Not only that, it's incredibly helpful later if someone asks for a particular video, and the file name doesn't include the name of the speaker. In that case, placing the name of the speaker in the title or author fields can be a lifesaver.

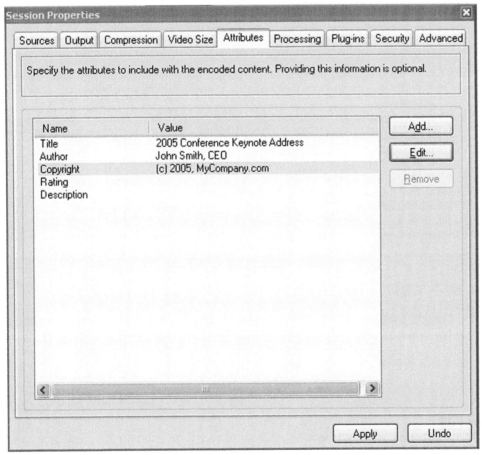

Figure 9-17
Use the title, author and copyright fields wisely.

Video Processing — Click the video processing tab to use the advanced filtering built in to the Windows Media Encoder (see **Figure 9-18**). This is where you can apply Inverse Telecine and Deinterlacing filters to your inputs. If you don't know whether your content requires these filters, you can use the Detect button to have the Windows Media Encoder sample your input and recommend filters for you to use.

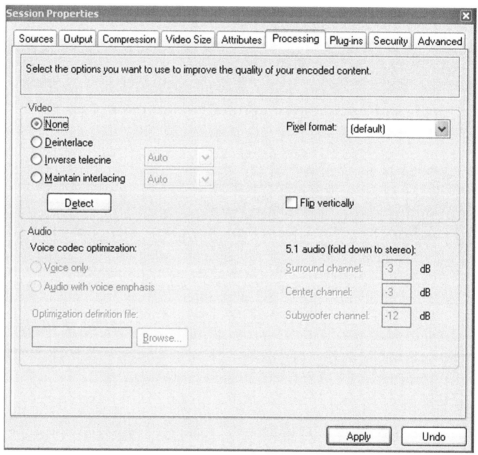

Figure 9-18
Use filters—but only if you need them.

Advanced Functionalities — There are a few more tabs available in the Properties window, but they offer advanced functionality that is not used very often, and specifically not covered in this book:

- **Plug-ins**: The Plug-ins tab enables you to do audio and video processing in the Windows Media Encoder. No processing plug-ins are included with the basic Windows Media Encoder install, you have to find third-party plug-ins and install them.

- **Security**: The Windows Media Encoder is capable of broadcasting files that are protected by digital rights management (DRM) schemes. This is a subject that warrants a book of its own.

- **Advanced**: You can do some harmless things on this tab, such as change the Identification name of the encoder or include time code in your file, and some incredibly dangerous things such as altering the maximum packet size. Don't touch it.

Apply Your Changes, Save the Session — Before you do anything, it's very important to click the Apply button in the bottom right corner of the Properties window. This registers all your changes, and will adjust the Windows Media Encoder interface accordingly. For example, if you're going to issue live script commands, a script panel will be displayed.

To save a session file, choose Save or Save As from the File Menu, and choose a location and file name for a session file. As always, using descriptive file names is a great idea.

Author's Tip

If you're using any kind of video input, chances are that the Windows Media Encoder is going to recommend that you use the Deinterlacing filter. However, if you're encoding at resolutions of 320 x 240 and below, don't bother. Streaming encoders discard one of the fields when the screen resolution is 320 x 240 or smaller, obviating the need for deinterlacing.

Author's Tip

Another good practice is to save an Encoder Session file. This file combines all the info you entered into the various tabs of the Properties window into a text file that can be opened up by any Windows Media Player. That way, if catastrophic failure should occur, you don't have to completely reconfigure your encoder—just double-click on the session file and go!

Start Encoding — If you're made it this far, there's nothing left to do other than to click the Start Encoding button at the top of the Windows Media Encoder. If there's enough room on your screen, the properties window will stay open, and your video inputs will be displayed, along with audio level meters. If there isn't enough room, your Properties window will automatically be closed to make room for the other panels of the encoder (see **Figure 9-19**).

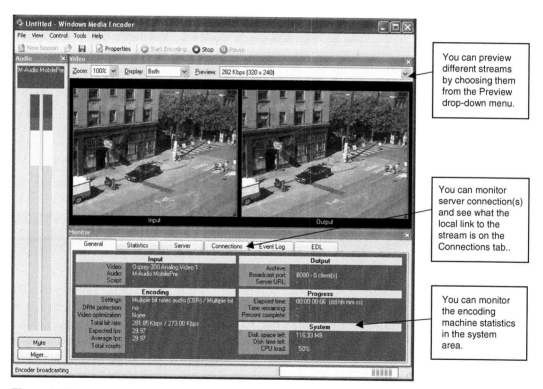

Figure 9-19
The Windows Media Encoder uses as much screen real estate as possible.

Test Your Stream — Just because your encoder is running doesn't mean your job is done. You've got to test your stream to make sure it's reaching the server and everything is working properly. The Windows Media server distributes live streams via publishing points. When you're linking to a live stream, link straight to the publishing point, using the following syntax:

rtsp://your.server.com/name_of_your_publishing_point

You can also link directly to the Windows Media Encoder. The link is displayed in the monitor panel of the encoder when you begin encoding, on the connections tab. It will look something like this:

http://123.34.67.89:8080

Checking your streams is probably the most important part of the whole process. Not only does it verify that the streams are actually available on the servers, but it also gives you a chance to see exactly what your audience is seeing. If you don't like what you're seeing, neither will they. Testing gives you a chance to adjust your settings if needed.

RealProducer

The RealProducer interface is similar to the Windows Media Encoder. The input is on the left, the output is on the right (see **Figure 9-20**). The bottom of the interface lists all the jobs that are scheduled, if you're using the encoder to do bulk encoding. To begin with, we need to set up our sources.

Figure 9-20
Most of the controls of the RealProducer are accessible from the main interface.

Selecting Sources — The RealProducer encodes from either files or devices. You can set up different sources for different jobs, and specify durations for jobs. You can't switch manually between sources like you can with the Windows Media Encoder. Click the radio button next to the type of source you want, and choose the source from the drop-down menu or click the Browse button if you're encoding from an archived file.

You should see your video source, and see audio level on the audio input meters. If you don't, there is something wrong with your sources. If you don't see your source listed in the drop-down menu, you may need to re-start the RealProducer, particularly if you're using a FireWire source and connected it after you started the RealProducer.

The Settings buttons next to the audio and video sources provide easy access to the audio input levels as well as any video controls that may be available. These will vary depending on your source and the capture card manufacturer.

Setting Up Your Outputs — The RealProducer encodes directly to files or to servers. To set up a live encode to a file, click the small RealOne icon underneath the destination pane. This pops open a standard "Save As" dialog box, where you specify a filename and click OK.

To set up a server destination, click the small server icon underneath the destination pane. This opens the server destination window (see **Figure 9-21**). At the top of this window, enter a name for the destination, the name of the live file, and select the broadcast method you'll be using.

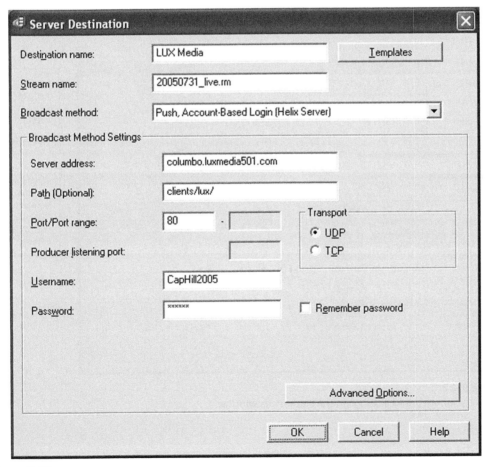

Figure 9-21
Enter your server details in the Server Destination window.

The RealProducer can do push and pull encoding, and supports a number of different account schemes. The one you choose will be dependent on the server setup and the onsite connectivity. Your distribution partner or IT department will provide you with the appropriate settings to use here. Be sure to save your settings as a template, as it makes setting up future webcasts easier.

Setting Up Audiences — The RealProducer calls a set of encoder settings an *audience*. Click on the Audiences button right above the destination pane to choose your encoding settings. This opens up the Audiences window (see **Figure 9-22**).

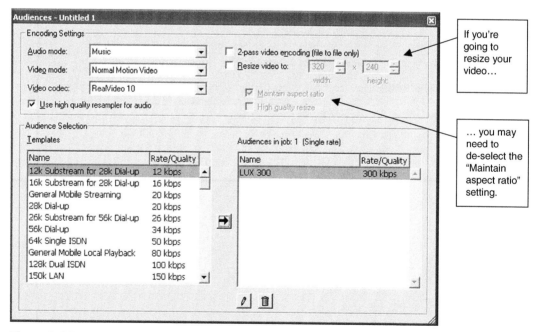

Figure 9-22
Choose your encoding settings in the Audiences window.

Starting from the top left, the first thing to choose is the type of audio codec to use. Use the voice codec only if you're absolutely sure your programming will not include music. Next, select your desired video quality by choosing an option from the Video mode drop-down menu. Finally, you can choose how much backwards compatibility you want by selecting which RealVideo codec you want to use.

> **ALERT** Backwards compatibility is only available with the RealProducer Plus. The RealProducer basic forces you to use the latest RealVideo codecs.

The right hand side is where you set the size of your output video. Click the "Resize video to:" checkbox to activate the resizing functionality. But beware—immediately below the resizing dimension specifications, there's a checkbox that means well but can get you into a whole lot of trouble.

The RealProducer defaults to having the "Maintain aspect ratio" check box checked when you enable the resize video functionality. In theory, this is a good thing. But in practice, it doesn't always work, because it doesn't take pixel geometry into account.

For example, if you're encoding directly from FireWire, the RealProducer senses that your input is 720 x 480. If you try to resize it to 640 x 480 while leaving the "Maintain aspect ratio" checked, you won't be able to. The box forces the mathematical ratio to remain constant; ignoring the fact that DV content uses different pixel geometry. The irony in this case is that the setting does exactly the opposite of what it is supposed to do.

However, it's easy to correct. Deselect the "Maintain aspect ratio" check box, and then type in 640 x 480 or 320 x 240, or whatever size you decide to use.

The bottom of this window is divided in half. The left side shows all available audience templates; the right side shows the templates that will be used for this job. Click the audiences you want and click the arrow between the two areas. Highlight audiences and click the trash icon beneath the right side to get rid of audiences you don't want.

Author's Tip

Remember, all audiences are forced to use the same screen resolution. If your audiences have radically different bandwidths available, it's probably a better idea to send them individual streams rather than compromise one for the other.

If you want to edit an audience, click the pencil icon underneath the Audiences window. This opens up the Audience Properties window (see **Figure 9-23**).

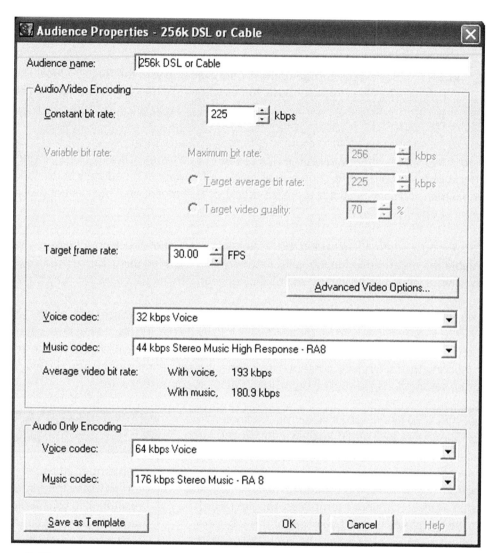

Figure 9-23
You can edit templates with RealProducer Plus.

You can change the total bit rate, the target frame rate, and the audio codecs used (depending on whether you specify music or voice on the Audiences page). There are also some additional settings available via the Advanced Video Options button, but unless you really know what you're doing, you probably shouldn't mess with these (see **Figure 9-24**).

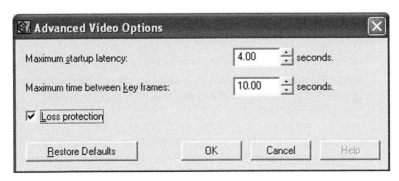

Figure 9-24
Use Loss protection to make your streams more robust.

One notable exception is the Loss protection setting. This builds in a little more redundancy into the file in case a packet is dropped along the way. Loss protection can make your file hold up a little better in some cases, and should always be used if you're encoding for the public Internet.

Of course, if you've made a number of changes it's a good idea to save your work as a template for next time.

Video Processing — Click the video filters button to access the video processing capabilities of the RealProducer. This opens up the Video Filters window, which provides cropping and black level correction, as well as deinterlace, inverse telecine, and noise filters. This window also features a video preview window.

The cropping interface does not provide any presets. Instead there are left and top crop values, and total height and width values that can be entered manually or adjusted by dragging the yellow bars in the video preview window. The preview window is a nice touch, but being sure you're maintaining a proper aspect ratio will involve some math.

Another interesting point is that the RealProducer does not stretch the cropped content to your specified resolution. If you need to crop your content and end up at a particular resolution, you have to start with a resolution that is larger than your target resolution, and crop accordingly.

For example, if you want to end up with a 320 x 240 resolution and want to crop off roughly five percent around the edges, then you'd have to set your resolution on the audiences page to 352 (320 plus ten percent) by 264 (240 plus ten percent). In the Video Processing window, you'd set the left parameter to 16, the top to 12, and the width and height to 320 and 240, respectively. Got it?

 ALERT Although the RealProducer will let you specify a larger output size than your input source, you cannot then crop this stretched video back down to your desired output size. The width and height settings on the cropping feature either override the settings on the Audiences page, or are ignored, depending on the order in which you set them.

The next processing feature available is black level correction. Black level correction makes the darkest areas of your screen black again. This helps restore the balance if you've adjusted your brightness, and also compensates for the difference between black on a television monitor and black on a computer monitor. Click the check box if you want to use this feature.

The final two (actually three) processing features available are deinterlacing/Inverse Telecine and Noise filtering. The Deinterlace/Inverse Telecine functionality is on by default—the RealProducer automatically uses it if it needs to. Finally, a noise filter is available if you have very low quality content.

Fill in Clip Information — Click the Clip Information button to fill in the title, author, and copyright information for your clip. (see **Figure 9-25**). As mentioned previously, this information is completely optional, but makes your webcast look far more professional. It also can be very helpful later on if you're looking for a particular piece of programming amongst a number of files that have unhelpful names.

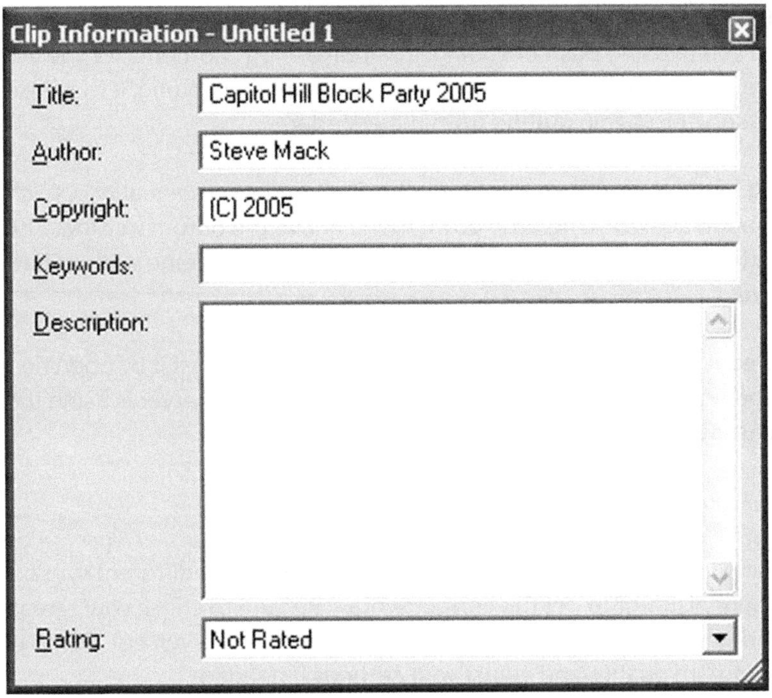

Figure 9-25
Fill in the clip information.

Save the Job File — Choose the Save Job option from the File menu to save all the encoding information for your webcast. Provided you're using a push encoding method, this job file can be copied to your backup machine(s) and used to fire up another encoder quickly if your main encoding machine suffers a catastrophic failure.

ALERT Unfortunately, saving job files is yet another option that is only available in RealProducer Plus.

Start Encoding — Click the Encode button at the bottom of the interface to start the encoding process. If you're using push encoding, it will take a few moments for the encoder to connect to the server and authenticate. If you're using pull encoding, it may take a few moments for the server to begin pulling from the encoder.

If you're using multiple audience templates, you can monitor the quality of each output by choosing the audience from the drop down menu above the output window. This is a handy feature that allows you to see what each of your audiences is seeing without having to open up a RealPlayer.

Test Your Stream — Don't forget to test your stream. You can test it by opening up a RealPlayer, and opening a connection directly to the server. If your server is using the default mount point, using the following syntax:

rtsp://your.server.com/encoder/name_of_your_file.rm

If you're running multiple servers, you may need to use slightly different syntax. Check with your system administrator to get the correct syntax. Be sure to check your streams on site. Not only is it important that the streams are available on the server, but also you'll be able to check your stream quality, and adjust your settings if needed.

Redundant Encoding Techniques

There are a number of approaches you can use to build redundancy into your webcast. The first, and most obvious, is to have multiple encoding machines available in case of equipment failure. However, there are other types of failure, and other techniques available to try and mitigate them.

For example, you might suffer a catastrophic connectivity outage. Using multiple connectivity paths is required to combat this. This requires using multiple encoding machines on different networks, and likely twice the connectivity fees.

Even if you don't use multiple connectivity paths, you can still send multiple feeds. If for some reason one of your encoders shuts down, the audience automatically rolls over to the backup feed, instead of being disconnected. This is a much better experience than having the audience wait until you restart the encoder or replace it with a backup machine.

Of course, to get this kind of behavior you need to provide access to the redundant streams using the redundancy features built in to your server platform or by using redundancy in your metafile. Server and metafile redundancy are covered in subsequent chapters.

Conclusion

Encoding involves some compromises in your stream quality, because the public Internet isn't yet capable of sustaining bit rates required for that level of quality. Therefore, consider your audience and type of programming when choosing your encoding settings.

You'll need powerful computers with good quality sound cards and capture cards or FireWire ports. Alternatively you can buy custom encoding solutions, or solutions dedicated to producing particular types of presentations.

Be sure to select the right audio codec, and allot a high enough audio bit rate to provide acceptable audio quality. Adjust your video resolution to optimize your video quality. Use video processing when you need it, being sure to always maintain the correct aspect ratio. After you've selected all your settings, save the templates or profiles, and the job file. Then, fire up your encoder and test your streams.

Finally, use as many redundant encoding techniques as you can afford to. The next chapter covers authoring, which is how you connect your audience to your content.

CHAPTER 10

Webcast Authoring

There are a number of ways of connecting your audience to your programming. The most important thing to consider when choosing a method is speed. People don't want to fill out forms, enter passwords, or spend ten minutes searching your website for the live stream. The best approach is to get them to the live stream as quickly and painlessly as possible.

This chapter starts with a general discussion of things you should be thinking about regarding your web page design, and then segues into the actual syntax for the various methods you can use.

- Authoring Considerations
- Standalone Players
- Embedded Players

Authoring Considerations

You have to consider two things when you're authoring for your webcast. First, how is the webcast going to be featured on the website? Is there going to be a link on the homepage, and will that link take people to an intermediate page, or directly to the webcast?

Second, you have to decide whether you're going to use an embedded player or offer a link that opens up a standalone player. Both methods have advantages and disadvantages. Of course, for redundancy purposes, you should offer both.

Regardless of which method(s) you use, you'll be using a text editor to place the link to your stream in a file, either a small text file known as a *metafile* or inside of special tags in an HTML file.

HTML Considerations

You should always try to put a link to your webcast on your home page. Webcasts tend to attract large audiences, all arriving at the same time. The first place they're going to go is your home page. This will place an abnormally large load on your web server. If your audience has to search through multiple pages to find the webcast, the load on the web server could be dangerously high.

This is bad for two reasons. First, the web server will slow down, making it even more frustrating for folks trying to find the webcast. Second, if the system load is too high, you run the risk of system failure. If your website fails, then no one will be able to get to your stream.

This is a good argument for keeping your website simple. It is not uncommon for people to simplify their websites if they're expecting huge crowds. Some organizations have even been known to replace their home page with a temporary home page that has a link to the web cast, and a link to the regular website.

It may sound extreme, but it works. The last thing you want is 10,000 people trying to download a fancy animation on your home page when all the audience wants to do is click the "skip intro" button. They're there for the webcast, not the animation. Furthermore, unless you've got programming that people are absolutely dying to see, it's not a good idea to force them to register.

Embedded vs. Standalone Players

There are two basic ways to present your webcast. You can either embed a streaming media player in a web page, or you can use links that pop up standard streaming media players. Many companies prefer the embedded approach because the experience is more seamless, since the webcast is seen in the context of the website, which has been carefully crafted and constructed to extend a company's brand.

Author's Tip

Registration pages, email addresses and passwords seem like a neat idea to the marketing department, but can frustrate viewers. If you must force people to register, message this well in advance of the webcast so people can take care of it in advance.

However, there can be issues when using embedded players. For embedded players to work properly, the audience's browsers and media players must be configured properly. Also, there are cross-platform issues, meaning that if you're trying to cater to people on the Mac or Linux platform, you may have some trouble.

Things have gotten much better for embedded players over the past few years. Using the right code, you can reach well over 90% of the average Internet audience with an embedded player. If you're working in a closed environment where you know exactly what software people are running, you should be able to make sure everyone can see your webcast.

The best approach in our experience is to offer an embedded player, with links to open up standalone players for folks who encounter problems with the embedded player. Using this approach you should be able to reach 100% of your audience.

Let's start with links to standalone players, since they're the simplest.

Standalone Players

Linking to standalone players has the advantage of being relatively foolproof. Provided people have the appropriate streaming media player installed, it will open up and start streaming the webcast.

However, you can't link directly to the webcast in your HTML code. To understand why, remember that browsers use the hypertext transfer protocol (HTTP) to communicate with web servers. Links to streaming media use the real time streaming protocol (RTSP)—which browsers do not understand. If you try to use an RTSP link directly in your HTML code in an anchor tag, the browser will display an error. What we need is a method to hand off the URL of the webcast directly to the streaming media player. This is done using what is known as a *metafile*.

Metafiles are small text files that are placed on web servers. They use special file extensions such as **.ram** and **.asx** that are uniquely associated with streaming media players. Because they're text files, they can easily be delivered via HTTP, which browsers understand.

When a browser receives a metafile, it hands off the file to the appropriate streaming media player. The streaming media player then opens the metafile, and extracts the URL to the stream. The process is illustrated in **Figure 10-1**.

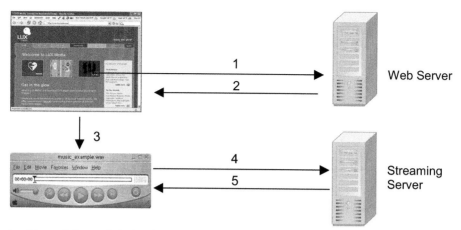

1. User clicks on link, issuing a request to a web server.
2. Web server returns a metafile.
3. Browser identifies metafile as belonging to a streaming media player, and hands it off to a streaming media application.
4. The player opens the metafile, extracts the URL, and issues a request to a streaming server.
5. The streaming server sends the stream to the player.

Figure 10-1
Use metafiles when you want to open up a standalone player.

Metafiles are a pretty simple solution, and work in almost all cases. One problem that can arise, though, is that they can be *cached*. Web servers and large content distribution networks (CDNs) use caching to speed up delivery of their most popular files. During a webcast, caching systems register that the metafile is very popular, and will cache them. This is great provided your metafile doesn't change, but if something goes wrong with your webcast and you are forced to change the URL of your webcast, the cached version will be out of date.

Also, chances are your webcast will use more than a single server. Therefore, you want spread your load across a number of different servers. Some distribution networks use hardware load balancing systems so an address like

> rtsp://my.streamingserver.com/2005Conference

is redirected to a number of servers automatically, without having to specify individual server names. Other systems, however, require different links for different servers. In this case, you need to dynamically generate your metafiles.

Dynamically generating metafiles is pretty simple, and something that any system administrator can take care of. Essentially, you generate the metafile on-the-fly, taking server load into account so that your load is evenly distributed amongst a number of servers.

Simple dynamic metafile generators assign requests to servers randomly; others actually monitor load levels and CPU usage to determine the optimal server to send the request to. However it is done, load balancing is essential for a successful webcast, and needs to be addressed when authoring metafiles. Work closely with your system administrators, and you'll be fine.

Metafile Examples

As mentioned previously, metafiles are very simple text files. Metafiles contain additional information about the file, most importantly the location, and information about how to play the file. The syntax varies from platform to platform, but the information they contain is basically the same.

Windows Media — Windows Media metafiles use an XML-based format, which means that tags are contained in angle brackets. It's similar to HTML (which is an XML-based language), but uses different tags. Here's a simple Windows Media metafile:

```
<asx version="3.0">

  <entry>

    <ref href="rtsp://your.wmserver.com/2005conference_live" />

  </entry>

</asx>
```

Let's go through this file line by line. The first line says that this is an **.asx** file, with the version number 3.0. The second line starts a new *entry*, which is a file and all the information that is associated with it. The third line is a reference tag that contains the URL of the actual stream. The fourth line closes the entry, and the final line closes the **.asx** file.

To use this code, simply type it into a text editor, substituting the correct URL in the <ref> tag, and save the file with an **.asx** file extension. Then place it on your web server, and link to the **.asx** file from the webcast web page. When the browser receives the **.asx** file, it will recognize it as belonging to the Windows Media Player, and hand it off accordingly.

There are a number of file extensions used by the Windows Media System, all of them ending in the letter "x." The idea is to use different file extensions for different types of streaming files, for example **.wax** for Windows Media Audio, and **.wvx** for Windows Media Video. When in doubt, use **.asx**, the generic version.

One thing to notice with XML files is that there are *unary* and *binary* tags. Unary tags are self contained, and always have a trailing slash before the closing angle bracket, like the <ref> tag above. Binary tags come in pairs, with the second, or closing tag, taking a slash *before* the tag name, i.e., </entry>. This syntax is common to all XML based metafiles.

The other thing to notice is how the file is indented. Indenting the file is not required but makes it easier to read, and more importantly, to debug when problems arise. For example, you could have quite a bit more information in your metafile:

```
<asx version="3.0">

  <entry>

    <ref href="rtsp://your.wmserver.com/file1.wmv" />

    <param name="title" value="Keynote Address" />

    <param name="copyright" value="2005 MyCompany.com" />

  </entry>

  <entry>

    <ref href="rtsp://your.wmserver.com/file2.wmv" />

    <param name="title" value="Thank you for coming." />

    <param name="copyright" value="2005 MyCompany.com" />

  </entry>

</asx>
```

In this case, there are two entries, each with two extra parameters. The Windows Media Player plays entries in **.asx** files in order, just like a play list. In this example, the two entries have different titles. There are many other parameters that can be used inside **.asx** files. For a full list, please consult the Microsoft website at:

http://msdn.microsoft.com/library/en-us/wcewmt/html/
_wcesdk_asx_asx_elements_reference.asp

RealMedia — RealMedia metafiles are plain text files, and take either the **.ram** or **.rpm** file extension. The ram file extension is used when you want the standalone RealPlayer to play the stream; the rpm file extension is used when you're authoring for an embedded player. A RealMedia metafile contains the URL to the stream, for example:

rtsp://your.realserver.com/YourStream.rm

Just type it into a text editor, save it with the right file extension, and put it on your web server. RealMedia metafiles can also take additional parameters, using the following syntax:

rtsp://your.realserver.com/YourStream.rm?parameter="value"&parameter="value"

To add additional parameters, simply put a question mark after the URL, and then the name of the parameter, an equals sign, and the value in quotes. Additional parameters can be added by adding an ampersand and then the parameter and value pair. For example:

rtsp://your.realserver.com/YourStream.rm?title="Conference 2005"&copyright="2005"

There are a number of parameters that can be used in RealMedia metafiles. Some parameters are tied to the file, such as title and copyright. Others dictate how the player displays the file, (for example screensize="full"), or what is displayed in the RealPlayer browser window. You can find more information about metafile parameters in the RealNetworks Production guide, available from the RealNetworks website:

http://www.realnetworks.com/resources/documentation/index.html

One last thing to note—**.ram** and **.rpm** files can have multiple entries, one entry per line. You can put comments in Real metafiles by placing a pound sign ("#") as the first character of a line. The RealPlayer plays through the files in order they're listed.

QuickTime — QuickTime metafiles use the **.qtl** (QuickTime Link) file extension, and are also XML-based files. A QuickTime link file looks like this:

```
<?xml version="1.0">

<?quicktime type="application/x-quicktime-media-link"?>

<embed src="rtsp://your.qtserver.com/YourStream.mov" />
```

The first two lines let the QuickTime player know that this is a link to a streaming file. The third file contains the URL of the actual stream. This example links directly to a QuickTime file. However, QuickTime broadcasts are slightly different, in that you must link to the *Session Description Protocol* file, which is a small file that is automatically created by the QuickTime broadcasting application.

The **.sdp** file must be placed on the QuickTime streaming server. Then, in the **.qtl** file, leave off the file extension of the **.sdp** file. For example, assuming you started a live QuickTime stream, and the broadcaster application created an **.sdp** file named keynote.sdp, you would load the keynote.sdp file onto your QuickTime server, and then the contents of your **.qtl** file would look like this:

```
<?xml version="1.0">

<?quicktime type="application/x-quicktime-media-link"?>

<embed src="rtsp://your.qtserver.com/keynote" />
```

It's a small difference, but it has to be done this way or it won't work. QuickTime link files can also take a number of parameters, which are added to the embed tag, using the following syntax:

```
<embed src="rtsp://your.qtserver.com/keynote" autoplay="true" fullscreen="true"

/>
```

A full discussion of QuickTime link file parameters is available on the apple website:

http://developer.apple.com/documentation/QuickTime/QT4WebPage/samplechap/special-11.html

ALERT Because the QuickTime link is a fairly recent innovation, you have to make sure your web server is configured to serve qtl files with the proper MIME type, which is:

```
.qtl = application/x-quicktimeplayer
```

Redundancy in Metafiles

As mentioned previously, the default behavior for metafiles is to behave like play lists, where entries are played in order. This enables the thoughtful reader to add a bit of redundancy to a webcast by placing multiple entries into the metafile. For example, consider the following RealMedia metafile:

rtsp://your.realserver.com/live_1.rm

rtsp://your.realserver_2.com/live_2.rm

rtsp://your.realserver.com/live_1.rm

rtsp://your.realserver_2.com/live_2.rm

The RealPlayer will attempt to play the first stream, live_1.rm, and continue to play it until the file finishes. If the file is unavailable, the RealPlayer will then attempt to play the second, and so forth. So if there are problems with live_1.rm, the player will "switch" to the second stream, and play that until it is finished or there is a problem.

You can achieve the same behavior with Windows Media **.asx** files by placing multiple <ref> tags in each <entry> tag. Also, because older versions of the player do not support RTSP, you may want to specify an alternative protocol:

```
<asx version="3.0">

   <entry>

      <ref href="rtsp://Server1/Path/File1.asf"/>

      <ref href="mms://Server2/Path/File1.asf"/>

   </entry>

</asx>
```

In this case, the player will attempt to connect via RTSP to the first stream, but if the player cannot connect via RTSP it will then attempt to connect to the second stream via MMS, the legacy Microsoft streaming protocol. You could also place multiple <entry> tags, each with multiple references.

Embedded Players

There is something irresistible about embedding a player in a web page that looks and feels like the rest of a website. The problem is that embedding a player requires different code depending on the browser, the OS, and the player version. Use the right code, and you've got a nice looking presentation. Use the wrong code, and you stand a good chance of shutting out a substantial portion of your audience.

As with most things relating to streaming, things have gotten considerably better in the last few years. Support across browsers has improved, as has support across operating systems. It's still not perfect, but using the techniques described in the following sections you should be able to embed a player that the majority of your audience will be able to see.

Author's Tip

For help on this chapter or any other chapters in the book, do not hesitate to contact the authors at *help@webcastingbook.com*.

The Microsoft ActiveX Control

Internet Explorer uses what is know as an ActiveX control to embed functionality into web pages. ActiveX controls are immediately recognizable by their use of the <object> tag. The following code embeds a QuickTime player:

```
<object classid="clsid:02BF25D5-8C17-4B23-BC80-D3488ABDDC6B"

    codebase="http://www.apple.com/qtactivex/qtplugin.cab"

    width="160" height="136" >

    <param name="src" value="rtsp://your.server.com/Conference2005.mov">

</object>
```

The first tag, the opening <object> tag, contains a few parameters:

- **classid**: The classid parameter is a unique string that identifies the object to be embedded, in this case the QuickTime player.
- **codebase**: The codebase parameter provides a URL for the user to link to if they do not have the required ActiveX control installed.
- **width, height**: These parameters specify the size of the embedded object.

The <param> tag contains a *name-value pair*, which means it contains a pair of parameters, specifying the name of and the value of the variable. In this case, it specifies the URL of the stream. There are additional parameters that can be specified in name-value pairs, such as whether the file should play automatically, whether to show the control bar, and many others, depending on which player you're embedding.

Author's Tip

It's good practice to also place a link to a metafile on the web page for folks who have problems with the embedded player.

The only problem is that Netscape-based browsers don't recognize the <object> or the <param> tags. To get compatibility across Netscape-based browsers, you need to use different code.

The Netscape Plug-In Model

Netscape-based browsers work similarly to Internet Explorer, but instead of an ActiveX control, they use what is known as a plug-in. Plug-ins use the <embed> tag:

```
<embed src="rtsp://your.server.com/2005Conference.mov" width="160" height="136"

    pluginspage="http://www.apple.com/quicktime/download/">

</embed>
```

The code is similar to the ActiveX code, but with all parameters included in the single <embed> tag:

- **src**: The src parameter specifies the URL of the stream
- **width, height**: The width and height parameters specify the size of the plug-in.
- **pluginspage**: The pluginspage parameter specifies the URL the viewer can go to if they do not have the required plug-in to view the webcast.

As with the ActiveX control, there are other parameters that can be included to specify various types of player behavior. The only difference is that they are included in <embed> tag as opposed to <param> tags.

Building Cross-Platform Web Pages with Embedded Players

Knowing what we do about embedding players in different browsers, how can we cater to both Internet Explorer *and* Netscape-based browsers? Thankfully, the answer is quite simple. We can cater to both by including the code for the Netscape Plug-in *within* the code for the ActiveX control. Take the following code for example:

```
<object classid="clsid:02BF25D5-8C17-4B23-BC80-D3488ABDDC6B"

    codebase="http://www.apple.com/qtactivex/qtplugin.cab"

    width="160" height="136" >

    <param name="src" value="rtsp://your.server.com/2005Conference.mov">

    <embed src="rtsp://your.server.com/2005Conference.mov" width="160"
height="136"

        pluginspage="http://www.apple.com/quicktime/download/">

    </embed>

</object>
```

The code begins with the <object> tag and code as per a standard ActiveX control. Then, the <embed> tag is included *within* the <object> tag. When Internet Explorer parses this code, it ignores the <embed> tag. Similarly, Netscape-based browsers don't recognize <object> or <param> tags, and ignore them.

Using this approach, you should be able to author pages with embedded players that the majority of your audience can see, provided they have the media player installed. The only time it gets tricky is with the Windows Media Player. There are a couple of reasons for this which are addressed next section.

Embedding the Windows Media Player

The Windows Media Player is embedded as a whole, just like the QuickTime player. The code looks pretty much the same:

```
<object classid="CLSID:6BF52A52-394A-11d3-B153-00C04F79FAA6"

    width="240" height="244" >

   <param name="url" value="media/wmv9.asx"/>

   <embed type="application/x-mplayer2"

     src="media/wmv9.asx" width="240" height="226">

  </embed>

 </object>
```

The <object> tag has the classid for the windows media player, and the standard width and height parameters, as well as a name-value pair specifying the URL of the file to be played. In this case, the URL is pointing to a metafile, with the standard **.asx** extension.

The <embed> tag, however, has a new addition: the type parameter. This must be included, and the value must be exactly as it is shown above. Other than that, the code is just as simple as the others. So why is embedding a Windows Media Player tricky? Well, there are a number of reasons:

- Microsoft discontinued support for the Netscape plug-in with the Windows Media 7.0 Player
- The 6.4 plug-in doesn't work on some Netscape browsers (6.x, 7.0)
- Internet Explorer on the Mac uses the Netscape plug-in, not the ActiveX control

However, just when all seemed lost, Windows Media resumed support for the Netscape plug-in with the Series 9 Player. Almost simultaneously, with version 7.1 Netscape began supporting the Windows Media Player ActiveX control. You can even download an extension for the open source Firefox browser to add Windows Media Player ActiveX support. So what's the problem?

The problem is that you don't know what browsers your audience will be using, or what version of the Windows Media Player they have installed. If they have Windows Media 9 or greater installed, chances are everything will be just fine, unless they're using Internet Explorer on a Mac. To further complicate the issue, the Windows Media Series 9 Player is only available for OSX.

It can all be a bit daunting, if you're trying to support every single possible permutation of browser, operating system, and player version. Using the code above, you stand a very good chance of reaching the majority of your audience. For those who have problems with the embedded player, offer a link to a metafile that opens up a standalone player, which hopefully will keep everyone happy.

Embedding the RealPlayer

The RealPlayer is embedded in pieces. Each piece of the RealPlayer you embed can be placed in a table, frame, or any valid HTML construct. In this example, we'll embed the video pane and all the controls, including the playback controls, the metadata window, and the status bar:

```
<!- code for Image Window -->

<object classid="clsid:CFCDAA03-8BE4-11cf-B84B-0020AFBBCCFA"

    width="240" height="180">

    <param NAME="controls" VALUE="ImageWindow" />

    <param NAME="console" VALUE="one" />

    <embed src="2005Conference.rpm" width="240"

        height="180" controls="ImageWindow" console="one" />

</object>


<!-- code for controls -->

<object classid="clsid:CFCDAA03-8BE4-11cf-B84B-0020AFBBCCFA"

    width="375" height="100">

    <param NAME="controls" VALUE="All"/>

    <param NAME="console" VALUE="one"/>

    <param NAME="src" VALUE="2005Conference.rpm"/>

    <embed src="2005Conference.rpm" width="375"

        height="100" controls="All" console="one" />

</object>
```

The first thing to note is that there are two separate blocks of code, each of which uses an <embed> tag within an <object> tag. The classid parameter is different, and is the string associated with the RealPlayer. Third, the code links to a metafile, but the metafile uses the rpm file extension. This is critical, because the Netscape plug-in uses file extension to determine what plug-in to use. The rpm file extension is registered to the RealPlayer plug-in.

There are two other parameters that are crucial to embedding the RealPlayer:

- Controls: The controls parameter determines what part of the RealPlayer is being embedded.
- Console: The console parameter is used to tie together all the different embedded pieces.

In the first block of code, the controls parameter is set to "ImageWindow." This is the part of the RealPlayer that displays video. The second block has the controls parameter set to "All," which embeds all the controls. Both chunks include the console parameter, which is set to "one." It doesn't matter what you set this parameter to, as long as it's set the same for all the embedded pieces of the RealPlayer.

You can actually embed multiple RealPlayers in a web page, and separate controls, as long as you use unique console parameters for each embedded player. As for the controls, the RealPlayer allows you to embed each control individually, or in groups. For full documentation of the RealPlayer, please refer to the RealNetworks Production guide, available from the RealNetworks website:

http://www.realnetworks.com/resources/documentation/index.html

 ALERT When embedding the RealPlayer, each <embed> tag must include the src parameter; however, only one of the <object> tags requires a source name-value pair.

Conclusion

When people watch a webcast, they're there for one thing: the webcast. So don't make them navigate through your entire site to find the link. Ideally, put a link on your home page. It's also a good idea to keep your site simple when you're expecting a big crowd. Webcasts put a strain on your web servers as well as your streaming servers.

The simplest way to connect your audience to your programming is to link to a metafile. Metafiles allow the browser to hand off to a player, either standalone or embedded. If you're going to use an embedded player, be sure to use both the <object> and the <embed> tags, so that both Internet Explorer and Netscape based browsers will be able to see your programming. It's also important to put a link to a metafile in case people have problems with the embedded player.

Next up is distribution. The final piece of software in the puzzle is the streaming server, which is the subject of the next chapter.

CHAPTER 11

Webcast Distribution

Now that you've invested the time and money to produce and encode a high-quality webcast, it's time to distribute it to the masses. This is where the Internet becomes a new mass medium, one without boundaries or licensing restrictions.

Thankfully, there is an existing web server infrastructure on the Internet, and streaming servers are not that different from web servers. There are a few ways in which they differ, and ways in which server hardware can be optimized for streaming, but basically the concept is the same: streaming servers respond to client requests for files. That's why it's important to leverage the experience of your network administrators—they understand how to build solid serving architectures.

This chapter covers the basics of streaming servers, and how you might want to set up your server architecture. In practice, you'll be working closely with your Network Administrators or working with a content distribution network (CDN) partner. No matter which approach you choose, it is helpful to understand how streaming servers operate. This chapter covers:

- Distribution Basics
- Distribution Techniques
- Server Setup Examples
- Log Files

Distribution Basics

Streaming servers are fairly simple. In a nutshell, they listen for requests from clients, and then fulfill them. The requests may be for an archived file, in which case they look to see if the file exists. In the case of webcasts, they look for a live stream or publishing point of the same name.

The main difference between streaming servers and web servers is that there is a persistent, two-way connection between streaming servers and players. If a viewer wants to pause the stream, the server must stop sending data. If the viewer wants to rewind or fast forward, the server needs to act accordingly. Of course, during a webcast these actions are not available, but nevertheless the functionality must be available.

Streaming servers therefore use different protocols than web servers. Whereas web servers use hypertext transfer protocol (HTTP), streaming servers use the real time streaming protocol (RTSP) or proprietary protocols such as Microsoft Media Services (MMS). These protocols are designed for the unique demands of streaming, which requires a two-way connection, and the ability to tightly control the data stream.

Streaming servers also offer additional functionality, such as the ability to build play lists, and the ability to insert advertising streams or banners. The feature sets vary from platform to platform. This chapter focuses on basic streaming server functionality, which is all you need to get your stream out to a large number of people. If you want to utilize the advanced functionality your server platform offers, you'll have to refer to your server documentation.

Size Matters

The first thing to consider when setting up your servers is the projected size of your audience. Streaming servers are very efficient and can easily service thousands of concurrent requests. You're more likely to encounter bandwidth issues than you are server resources issues.

For example, let's assume we're expecting an audience of 500 viewers, and we're serving broadband streams at 300 Kbps. That's nearly 150 Mbps. If your servers have 100 Mbps network cards in them, as most do, you'd hit your ceiling somewhere in the vicinity of 250–300 users. If you're using gigabit Ethernet, this would bump up to 2,500–3,000 users. This is because each stream will have some overhead associated with it, and the practical maximum load on a network is 60% to 70% of the theoretical capacity.

If we assume your server has a 100 Mbps network card, it's easy to see you're going to need multiple servers for this webcast. If your server has a gigabit Ethernet card, you could service your audience with a single server. Of course, you should always have *at least* two servers, for redundancy purposes.

Running a single streaming media server is well within the reaches of anyone who reads this book. Running a well-balanced, multiple location server array may not be. These days, many streaming media providers choose to use a third party to host their webcasts. Large-scale streaming providers have the infrastructure, the bandwidth, and the experience required for large webcasts.

Even if you're going to outsource your webcast distribution, it's important to understand how the process works, so that you understand exactly what third parties are offering. Also, when something goes wrong, you'll be able to figure out if it was something you did—or if it was your distribution partner.

Equipment

Streaming software can run on virtually any computer, though it's best to have a server-class machine. Server-class machines are built to withstand years of continuous performance. Streaming servers should also have plenty of RAM, because each stream needs a small amount of dedicated RAM to keep the process open. Start with a Gigabyte of RAM and work your way up from there.

Since you're going to be running a number of streaming servers, you'll need a way to load balance across the machines. This can be done using hardware or software. If you already have load-balancing hardware for your web servers, this equipment can be used to load balance your streaming servers. You also can load balance via virtual servers such as the Linux Virtual Server, or a simple script.

Platforms

QuickTime, Windows Media, Real, and Flash all have mature server platforms. The platform you choose will depend on a number of issues:

- **Audience**: If your audience is a known quantity, you may lean towards a particular player, and therefore the corresponding server.

- **Server Features**: Some server platforms, most notably Windows Media and Real, offer more functionality that is tailored to webcasting.

- **Operating System**: If your organization has standardized on a particular OS, you may need to choose your server accordingly.

- **Stream Quality**: While all streaming platforms offer acceptable audio and video quality, the quality of Windows Media and RealMedia currently exceeds that of QuickTime and Flash.

Author's Tip

The Helix server from RealNetworks can serve live Real, Quick-Time, and Windows Media streams. The Helix server cannot, however, serve Windows Media 9 Series MBR files.

If you're going for maximum coverage, it's usually a good idea to offer at least two formats. This may involve running two streaming platforms, but might be worth it if you're trying to reach every last audience member. This is another reason why using a third party to host your webcast is a good idea.

Distribution Techniques

After you decide on the platform (or platforms) you'll be using, it's time to think about your server architecture. You're going to need multiple servers—that much you know. But how will they be deployed? Will they be co-located at a single ISP, or will they be geographically dispersed? How will traffic be distributed across the servers?

The answers to these questions depend largely on the scale of your broadcast, and your budget. Ideally, you want geographically dispersed servers, for two reasons. First, having the servers in different locations on different network segments gives you redundancy if one of the data centers suffers catastrophic failure. Second, your audience may get better stream quality if they're physically closer to the server.

There is some disagreement as to whether quality improves when the stream has a shorter distance to travel. The problem is not the distance the data has to travel; rather it's the traffic that the stream may encounter, or a faulty router that may be overloaded or dropping packets. If there's a traffic problem between you and the streaming server, it doesn't make a bit of difference where the server is located. However, statistically speaking, having servers in a number of locations certainly reduces the probability of problems.

Regardless of where they're located, you're going to need more than one, and therefore the live stream will have to be distributed to all the servers. If you're running redundant encodes from the site, you may want to send them to two different servers, for even more redundancy. **Figure 11-1** illustrates what a redundant server architecture might look like.

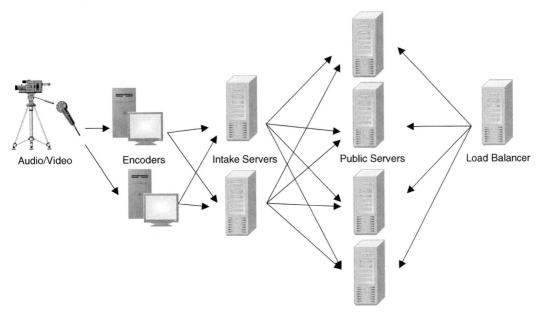

Figure 11-1
A highly redundant webcast infrastructure.

In **Figure 11-1**, two encoders each feed two different intake servers. The intake servers then feed public servers, creating a web of connections that make this setup highly redundant. Depending on which streaming platform you are using, you would either use metafile redundancy, load balancing, or the redundant features built in to the server.

Live Server Redundancy

Webcasts require a redundant server architecture, that much is clear. All the major streaming platforms offer the ability to create redundant architectures, but use different terminology when they describe it.

- Redundancy on the QuickTime platform is described in terms of *relays*. Any QuickTime server can act as a relay, forwarding a live stream to other servers.

- RealServer redundancy is described using the concept of *splitting*. Any RealServer can act as a *transmitter*, sending the stream to other servers configured as *receivers*.

- The Windows Media system describes live broadcasts in terms of *publishing points*. A publishing point can have an encoder as its source, or another server.

Redundant server architectures usually consist of a number of *origin* or *ingress* servers that receive incoming encoded streams from encoding software. These servers distribute the streams to *public* servers, which service requests from the audience. The public servers can be coincident with the origin servers, or in completely different locations. The complexity of your architecture is dependent only on your imagination.

Setting up your redundant architecture requires configuration of both the origin servers and the public servers. The origin servers have to be configured to either *push* streams to public servers, or to allow public servers to *pull* streams from them. Similarly, public servers have to be configured to allow incoming streams from origin servers, or to request the necessary streams from the origin servers.

Depending on the platform you're using, you may have to set certain permissions, fill in IP addresses here and there, and specify other necessary parameters. This is easily taken care of via the administration interface provided by your platform, or via a configuration file. Examples of this are given later in this chapter in the "Distribution Examples" section.

After you've set up your redundant architecture, you'll need some form of load balancing to take advantage of it. Load balancing can be done via hardware or software, using varying degrees of intelligence. For example, some load balancing techniques take into account the processor load on each machine when determining which server to send a request to. Others take geography or network paths into account, while some simply use randomization to distribute the load.

Author's Tip

If you have existing load balancing hardware or software for your web servers, it can probably be used for your streaming servers with a few modifications.

Deployment Considerations

Figure 11-1 illustrates what a redundant webcast server architecture might look like, but says nothing about where the servers are located. The public servers could be located in the same ISP, or geographically dispersed. The physical location of your servers will depend on the audience you're trying to cater to, and of course budget. Another consideration is the type of broadcast you're doing: unicast or multicast.

Unicast vs. Multicast — Most webcasts are delivered via unicast delivery (see **Figure 11-2**), where each audience member is sent a unique copy of the stream. This is particularly inefficient during webcasts, because each audience member must be sent a unique copy of the stream, even though they're all watching the same programming. A more efficient delivery method known as multicasting can be used to reduce the number of outbound streams.

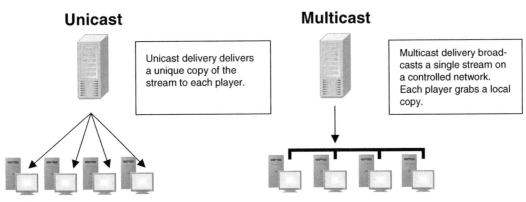

Figure 11-2
Unicast vs. multicast delivery.

Multicast distribution is similar to traditional broadcasting methods. Using multicast, a single stream is sent across a network. Audience members grab a copy of the data instead of having a unique copy sent to them. This approach can reduce traffic levels drastically.

Although in theory multicasting sounds fantastic, in practice multicasting is not yet feasible on the public Internet. Multicast requires all routers on the network to be multicast-enabled, and for all routers to pass all multicast traffic. The problem is the Internet is a widely-dispersed resource with thousands if not millions of people controlling different network segments, and not everyone wants stray multicast traffic on their networks.

Multicasting should be used in closed environments such as corporate LANs. If you're doing an internal broadcast, it's quite simple to do it as a multicast. Not only does it cut down on your LAN traffic, but also since the traffic load is lower, you can afford to encode at a higher bit rate. Internal multicasts should target bit rates in the 700 Kbps–1 Mbps range. This provides enough quality for full screen, full frame rate webcasts.

Hybrid approaches can be used to take advantage of multicasting where it makes sense. For example, **Figure 11-1** could include servers that are situated on multicast-enabled networks. Each of those servers would receive a single unicast stream, and then multicast the stream to a local area network.

Live Stream Latency — One drawback to creating redundant server architectures is an increase in stream *latency*. Latency is the difference between when an event happens and when the broadcast audience actually sees or hears it. Typical webcasts may have latencies of 15–30 seconds.

The latency occurs for a number of reasons. First, the encoder encodes in near real-time, but not instantaneously, so a small amount is due to the time it takes to encode. The second culprit is the origin server. Servers buffer the incoming streams as a protective measure against network traffic or dropped packets. If you have a highly redundant architecture, with multiple levels of servers, each server will add latency to the stream.

In many cases, latency is not a problem, because the audience is unaware of it. However, in situations where there needs to be audience participation, latency is a big problem. There's not much you can do about it. If latency is a big issue, then the commercial streaming media platforms are probably not the best answer for you.

Firewalls — Firewalls protect computers from intruders and hackers by monitoring the traffic to and from your servers. Typically firewalls are configured to accept incoming traffic on a limited set of ports, and using a limited set of protocols. Webcast professionals have to worry about a number of different firewalls: the firewalls that may be protecting the distribution servers, the firewalls that the encoders may be behind, and finally the firewalls that the audience members are most likely behind.

If you're using a firewall to protect your streaming servers, be sure to open up the required input and output ports, and be sure to allow the right kind of traffic. The ports used vary between streaming platforms, but generally include port 554 for RTSP traffic, port 80 for HTTP traffic, and a number of ports for communication between servers, players, and other servers.

If you're encoding at a remote location and you're behind a firewall, you'll most likely have to use the push method of encoding, because firewalls generally don't allow remote servers to pull data from behind the firewall. There are exceptions, but they generally involve a bit of advanced configuration on the firewall. Usually it's easier to just use push encoding.

ALERT If your audience is behind a firewall, they will most likely be blocking RTSP traffic, which most firewalls do by default. Streaming servers are aware of this, and do what is known as *protocol rollover* to mitigate the problem. Using protocol rollover, a streaming server will first attempt to send data via RTSP on port 554, and if it does not receive acknowledgement from the player, then it "rolls over" to RTSP packets sent via TCP/IP on port 80. If this fails, the final option is to send packets via HTTP.

Webcasting "Canned" Performances

Knowing all you do about the complexity of webcasts, the question has to be asked: "Does it have to be live?" We're not necessarily talking about the experience the audience has. For example, many "live" events on television are actually produced hours if not weeks in advance, and then simply broadcast "live." To the audience, the experience is the same.

Streaming media servers enable the exact same functionality. You can produce an entire program, polish and edit it as you like, and then "webcast" it at a predetermined time. As far as the audience is concerned, the event is live, but it reduces the complexity and the risk of a truly live webcast by orders of magnitude:

- You don't need encoding equipment on site

- You don't need connectivity on site

- If you mess up, you can do another take, and edit

- If equipment fails, you can fix it, and do another take

Windows Media Services enables simulated broadcasts by using a single file or a play list as a source for a broadcast publishing point instead of an encoded stream. When the publishing point is started, the server automatically begins serving the play list, and the simulated broadcast begins.

The RealServer provides a small software application called the G2SLTA (simulated live transfer agent) that plays back encoded streams and sends them to a server as if it were an incoming live stream. The G2SLTA can be run on the same machine as the server, or on a remote machine. The G2SLTA simulates the broadcast of a single file or a list of files, however, if you're using a play list, the files must have been encoded using the same settings.

The QuickTime server provides simulated live broadcasts via the Playlist Broadcaster application. The Playlist Broadcaster can simulate broadcasts of single files or play lists. When using play lists, all files must be encoded using the exact same settings.

Server Setup Examples

All streaming servers run based on settings that are read from a configuration file. The Windows Media Services and RealNetworks Helix platforms offer interfaces that enable an administrator to configure the server remotely. This makes server setup easy, and remote troubleshooting and problem solving much simpler.

Most streaming server software is ready to run as soon as it is installed. You must set up an administrative account and accounts for any other people who will be using the server. You also may want to configure the server as part of a redundant architecture, in which case you'll need to configure whether the server is relaying streams to other servers, or using other servers as a source.

RealNetworks Helix Server

The Helix server provides a simple web-based interface for all administrative tasks (see **Figure 11-3**). The first thing you'll want to do is configure all your ports. This interface is available via the Server Setup menu option on the left side. In most cases it's best to use the default values, because other applications such as encoders and firewalls may assume certain known ports.

There are a number of other general parameters you can set up in the Server Setup section, but most of these can be left with their default settings. Click on the Broadcasting link on the left for webcast setup (see **Figure 11-4**). The Helix server is capable of webcasting Real, QuickTime, and Windows Media streams, and offers a separate screen of options for each.

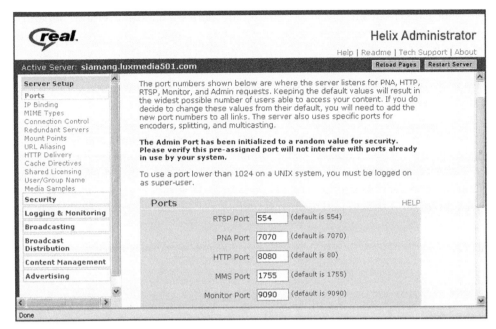

Figure 11-3
Configure your ports via the Helix Administrator.

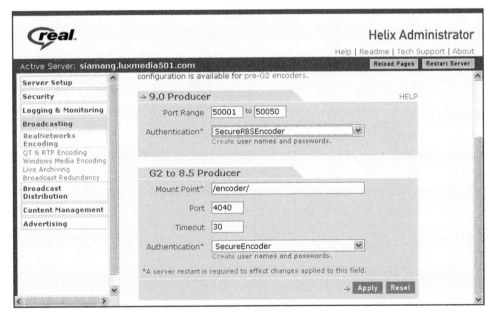

Figure 11-4
The Helix server options for RealProducers.

If you're webcasting Real streams via a Helix server, there are different settings depending on what version of the encoder you're running. Legacy encoders require a port number (which defaults to 4040), and default to a *mount point* of *encoder*. This means that all your live streams will appear in a directory named encoder. You can change this on this screen if you want. You also can specify an authentication mode on this screen, and create usernames and passwords.

The Helix server also has configuration pages for QuickTime broadcasts and Windows Media broadcasts. On the Windows Media configuration page, you can specify a mount point for Windows Media broadcasts, as well as information about the source encoder (see **Figure 11-5**). The Helix server only supports pull encoding, and therefore requires the IP address and port from which it should pull the live stream.

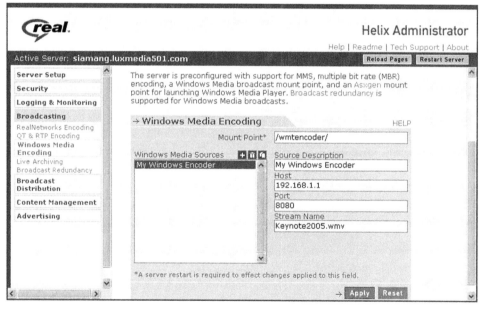

Figure 11-5
Enter the Windows Media Encoder information for Windows Media broadcasts.

An interesting feature provided by the Helix server is broadcast redundancy (see **Figure 11-6**). Broadcast redundancy enables the Helix server to accept more than one source for a live stream. If one stream should fail, the server will automatically switch to another stream as the source. The configuration enables you to configure the behavior of this functionality.

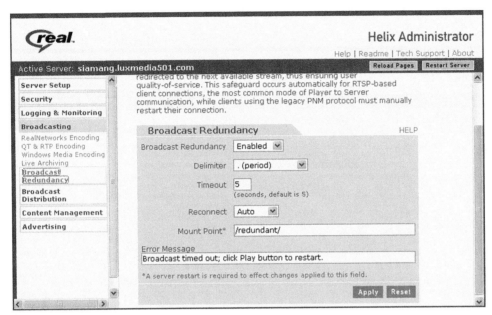

Figure 11-6
Configure the broadcast redundancy.

For server redundancy, you have to set up your servers as transmitters and receivers. These settings are available from the Broadcast Distribution option on the left side (see **Figure 11-7**). To configure a transmitter, you have to specify at least one receiver to which the server should send streams. You can specify which streams to distribute by specifying a particular mount point. Any streams encoded to that mount point will automatically be distributed to all the receivers. You also must specify the IP address or hostname of the receiving server.

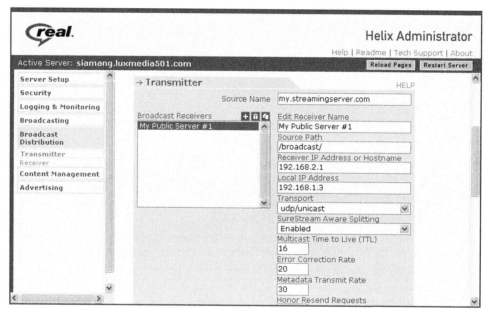

Figure 11-7
Configuring a Helix server as a transmitter.

Be sure to scroll down on this screen, as you have to make a note of what port range and what type of security the transmitter will use. The receiver must be configured to use the exact same port range and security type, or the distribution will fail.

To configure a Helix server as a receiver, click on the Receiver menu option on the left under Broadcast Distribution. The receiver screen is very similar to the transmitter screen (see **Figure 11-8**). You must specify the transmitters that are allowed to send streams to the server, the port range they'll be using, and the security type, which may require a username and password.

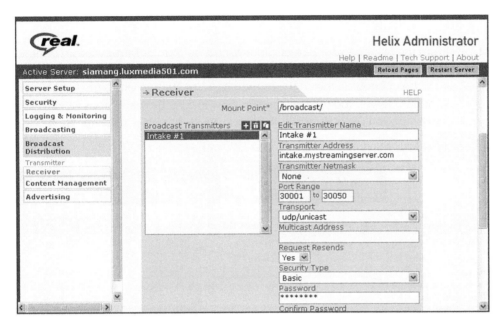

Figure 11-8
Configuring a Helix server as a receiver.

There are many other configuration options available via the Helix Administrator. There is also a live monitor that enables you to monitor server performance in real time. This can be handy for troubleshooting, and for getting a rough idea of how many people are connected to your webcast.

A full discussion of all the configuration options of the Helix server is beyond the scope of this chapter. For more information, please refer to the documentation that is available from the RealNetworks website:

http://www.realnetworks.com/resources/documentation/index.html

Windows Media Services

Windows Media Services is available as part of the Windows Server software. Before you configure your streaming server, make sure the operating system and the required services are configured appropriately. You can do this by checking the current settings against the default service settings in the Windows Server Help and Support Center.

Setting up a Windows Media server is done via a wizard.

1. From the Manage Your Server window, choose "Add or remove a role" (see **Figure 11-9**). The Manage Your Server window should already be open, but if not it can be opened via the control panel. If you're starting with a fresh install of Windows Server, you may be confronted with a Preliminary Steps window; if so make sure you've satisfied all the necessary steps before clicking "Next."

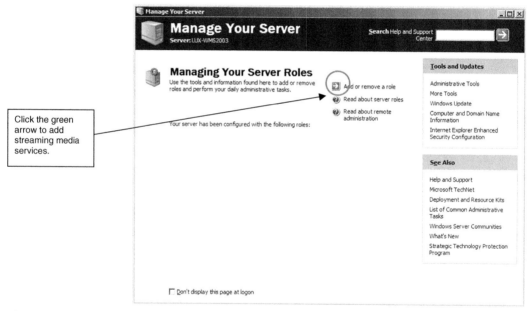

Figure 11-9
To add streaming services, add a "role" to your Windows Server.

2. The server then analyzes what services are already running. If you're working on a new install, you can either set up a default common set of options, or use the custom configuration method to set up a single service, in this case a streaming server. The safest option is always to set up the *minimum* amount of services. In this example, we'll assume we're only setting up a streaming server. Choose the "Custom configuration" method.

3. Eventually you should see the Server Role window (see **Figure 11-10**). Highlight the Streaming media server option and click "Next."

4. This brings up a screen where you confirm your selection. Click "Next." The Windows Media server then pops up a widow and automatically installs and configures your Windows Media Server. No feedback is required from you.

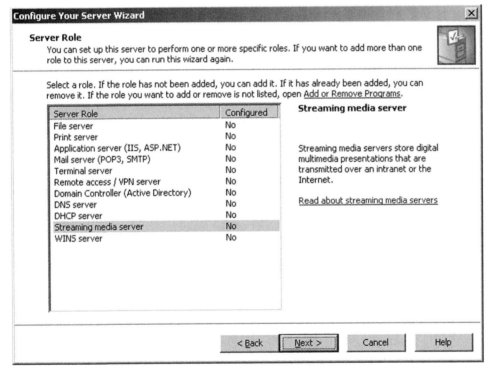

Figure 11-10
Adding a Streaming server "role" to your Windows Server.

5. When the Windows Media Server has been installed, the pop-up window will display a success message (see **Figure 11-11**). Click the Finish button. You should now see a Streaming Media Server listed in the Manage This Server window.

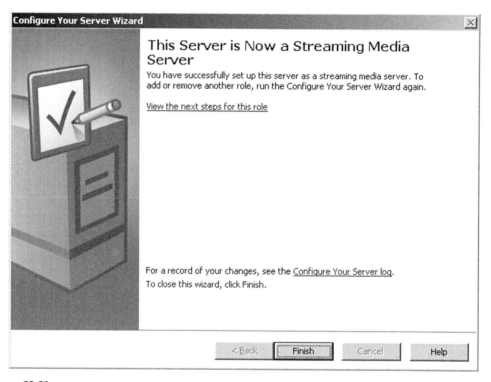

Figure 11-11
Congratulations! You've installed Windows Media Services.

Now that you have a server installed, you need to configure a publishing point for your webcast.

1. From the Manage This Server window, choose the "Manage this streaming server" link. This opens up the Windows Media Services management window. This is where all the day to day management and administration of your Windows Media services takes place.

    This page lists the name of your server, and whether or not it is running (or "started" in Windows Media-speak). You can test your server on this page, monitor the hardware performance, and see who is connected to your server.

2. In this case we'll create a publishing point by clicking on the "Create a broadcast publishing point" link (see **Figure 11-12**). This opens up the Add Publishing Point Wizard.

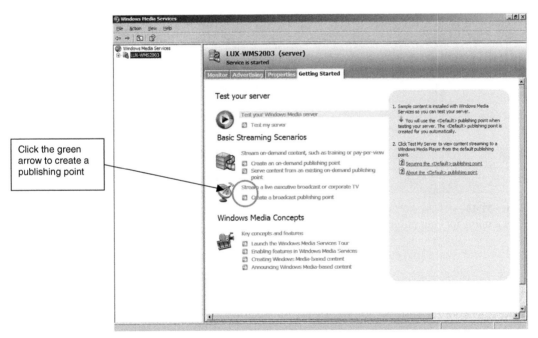

Figure 11-12
Click the green arrow next to "Create a broadcast publishing point" to set up your webcast.

3. The Add Publishing Point Wizard walks you through the simple process of setting up a publishing point. Click "Next" to get through the welcome screen, and then enter a name for your publishing point on the next screen (see **Figure 11-13**).

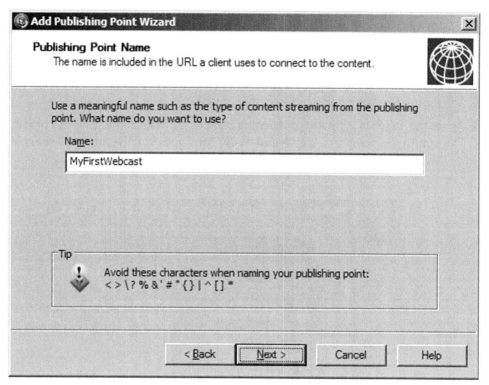

Figure 11-13
Enter a name for your publishing point.

4. Next, specify the source for your live stream. You'll see that the Windows Media Server enables you to use different types of sources, easily enabling rebroadcasts of previously recorded files, or broadcasts of play lists (see **Figure 11-14**). Choose your source and click "Next."

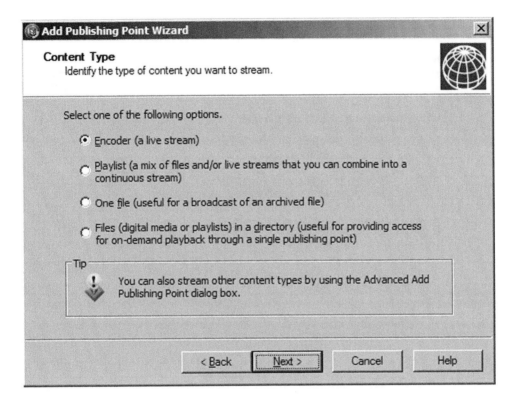

Figure 11-14
Choose the source for your webcast.

5. The next screen asks what type of playback scenario you want to create (see **Figure 11-15**). For webcasts, you want to create a Broadcast Publishing point. Some source options only enable this option; others enable you to create on-demand publishing points. Choose "Broadcast publishing point" and click "Next."

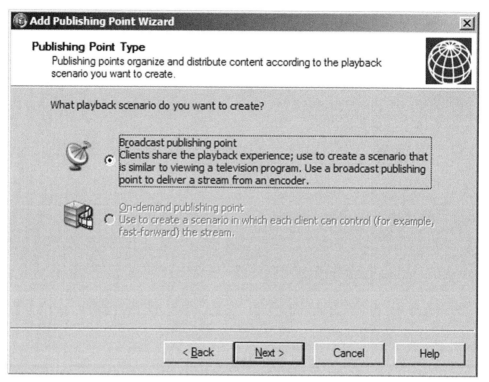

Figure 11-15
Choose "Broadcast publishing point" for your webcast playback scenario.

6. Next it's time to choose a delivery option. If you're webcasting on the public Internet, choose "Unicast." If you're webcasting on a multicast-enabled network, you can use multicast to reduce network traffic. You can enable multicast with unicast rollover and cater to both audiences, but this may cause some delay while the Windows Media Player rolls over to unicast. For most applications, Unicast is the easiest approach (see **Figure 11-16**).

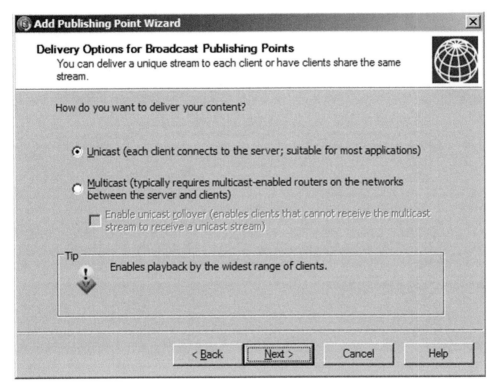

Figure 11-16
Choose your delivery option.

7. The next window is where you specify the address of your encoder. For pull encoding, you must have a hard-coded IP address for the Windows Media Encoder. Your encoder will display the IP address and port number it is expecting connections on. This must match the information you enter here (see **Figure 11-17**).

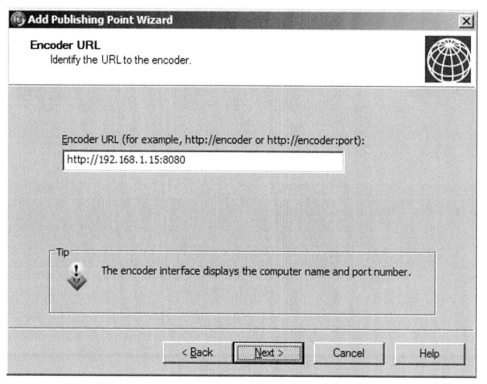

Figure 11-17
Enter the IP address of your encoder for pull encoding.

ALERT The IP address displayed in **Figure 11-17** is a local network address and will only work if your encoder and server are on an internal LAN. You should use a routable IP address in most cases.

8. Next the wizard asks if you'd like to enable logging on your publishing point (see **Figure 11-18**). You should always enable logging so you can keep track of who is watching your webcast, and for how long.

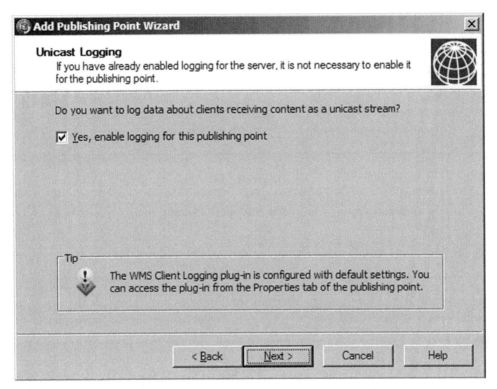

Figure 11-18
Always enable logging for your webcasts.

9. The penultimate screen of the publishing point wizard is a summary, displaying all the settings you just entered (see **Figure 11-19**). You also have the option on this screen to automatically start the publishing point as soon as the wizard is finished. Provided everything looks right, you can click the next button.

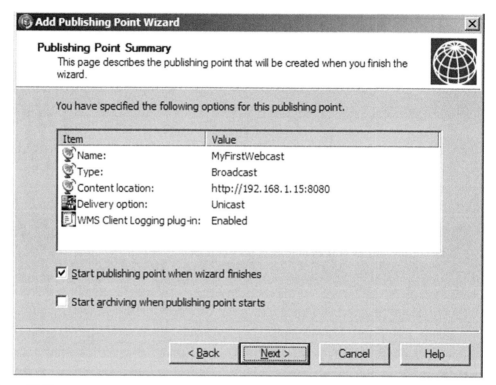

Figure 11-19
Click the "Start publishing point when wizard finishes" to enable your publishing point.

10. The final screen offers you the option of automatically creating a metafile or web page for your webcast. If you choose to have the server create a metafile for you, make sure the URL in the metafile is a fully qualified URL. The wizard defaults to using a local URL, such as:

mms://Server2003/MyFirstWebcast

This will not be a valid URL for anyone outside of your local server domain. Your URL should use a fully qualified URL or IP address, such as:

mms://server1.mydomain.com/MyFirstWebcast

11. Once you start your publishing point, the server establishes a connection to your source, and your webcast is live. If you need to change anything about your publishing point, or indeed make any changes to your server, you can choose the appropriate selection from the tree of options on the left side. For instance, choose your publishing point from the left hand tree, and then choose the Properties tab (see **Figure 11-20**). On this page, you can modify all the settings for your publishing point.

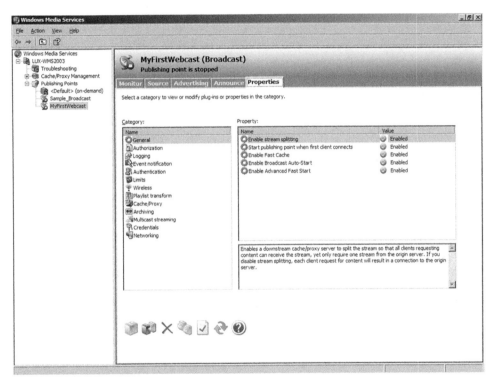

Figure 11-20
Modifying your publishing point settings.

12. This is where you set up redundancy. On your origin server, you'd want to make sure that stream splitting was enabled on the Properties page. For your distribution servers, you'd click on the Source tab of your publishing point properties, and click on the Change button, which pops up the Change Content Source window (see **Figure 11-21)**. Type in the URL for the remote broadcast point, and the server will pull live streams from the origin server.

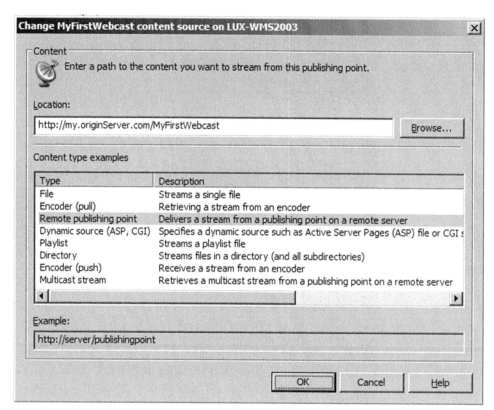

Figure 11-21
Specify a remote publishing point to set up redundant server architectures.

There are a myriad of other configuration options available via the Windows Media Server. There is ample documentation on the Microsoft website, and the server comes with a built-in help system that can help you through most configuration options. For the most part, they're simple to figure out, using the helpful wizards.

Log Files

Once you've successfully completed your webcast, the first question on everybody's lips will be, "How many people were watching?" If you're using a third party to handle your distribution, you may have access to real-time statistics that provide you with instant answers. If you're distributing your own streams, you'll find your answers in the log files.

Each time a streaming server processes a request from a client, it makes an entrance into a log file. The log file syntax varies from server to server, but at a minimum includes the following information:

- IP address of the client
- Date and time of the request
- The path and filename of the request
- The amount of data that was transferred

Depending on the platform you're using, you may also have additional information in your log files such as the protocol used, the bit rate of the stream, the player version, and a number of other interesting tidbits. By analyzing this information, you can determine who is watching your webcast, which bit rate they're watching, and how long they're watching.

There are a number of programs available to analyze log files. Many web server log file processing programs are adding modules that allow them to process streaming server log files:

- AWStats
- Sawmill
- FunnelWeb

You should use the information you get out of your log files to refine your webcasting efforts. For instance, if your webcasts are 30 minutes long but the average viewer only watches for 10 minutes, then you need to think about your programming. You should be able to find out what player versions people are using to connect to your streams, which may enable you to upgrade the codec you're using for your webcasts.

You also can get feedback about your distribution architecture from the log files. If many people are connecting from a certain geographic area, it might make sense to locate a server in their area for better performance. You also can look at error logs to see which servers are having the most problems, and why. Log files provide a wealth of information, and should be used to figure out how you can make your webcasts better.

Conclusion

Streaming servers used for webcasts don't need heavy-duty processing power, but it never hurts to have a server class machine with plenty of RAM. Webcast serving architectures must be redundant. The amount of redundancy will depend on the scale of your webcast. You should always have at least one intake server and two public servers.

All streaming platforms offer good quality and robust performance. Your choice of streaming platform will probably have to do with your audience, your existing server infrastructure, and the feature set of the server.

Given the complexity of a webcast, you should consider whether it is possible to record the event in advance and then webcast it using a simulated webcast at a later time. Although it doesn't offer the excitement of a truly live event, the audience may not notice the difference, and the reduced number of requirements makes it a worthy alternative.

CHAPTER 12

Case Studies

This chapter is where "the rubber hits the road;" where actual webcasts are dissected to give you a window into how the information in this book translates into actual situations.

This chapter presents three case studies, each with a slightly different twist. Depending on your situation, you may find one of these to more closely match what you're trying to achieve. Each one has nuances that you're bound to find useful:

- X-Prize Competition
- ACLU Members Conference
- Sweet Adelines Convention

For additional webcasting case studies and return on investment articles, please visit *www.streamingmedia.com/research/center.asp?id=2*

X-Prize Competition

The X PRIZE foundation (*www.xprize.org*) is a non-profit group that offered a $10 million prize to jump-start the space tourism industry through competition among the most talented entrepreneurs and rocket experts in the world. The prize would be awarded to the first privately financed team that designed a private spaceship that successfully launched three humans to a sub-orbital altitude of 100 km (62 miles) on two consecutive flights within two weeks.

In October of 2004, SpaceShipOne, designed and built by legendary airplane designer Burt Rutan and his team at Scaled Composites (*www.scaled.com*), made the first official attempt to win the X PRIZE award. Knowing that this event would be of interest to people all over the world, the X PRIZE foundation chose to webcast the event.

Implementation

The A/V feeds were taken from the on-site production that was there to document the event. The video feed included video from cameras on the ground, in the space ship, on the event stage and from other locations. The encoded streams were sent back to the content delivery network (CDN) via three bonded T1 lines, then distributed by the CDN Mirror Image Internet, a global provider which delivered it from the US, Europe and Asia.

For encoding, a "road-encode" box made by Globix, a webcasting services company based in NYC, was used. The road-encode includes multiple hardware encoders; flat panel monitor, audio/video splitters and everything you need to broadcast live on the Internet. All you need is power and an Internet connection.

Significant amounts of redundancy had to be built-in to this webcast because of its remote location. To start with, there were redundant hardware encoders in the road-encode unit. Additionally, a satellite truck was on site and available if needed. Backup Internet connectivity was provided by a WanderPod.

The WanderPod (*www.wanderport.com*) is a communications device that offers 2-way satellite uplink, Wi-Fi, and VoIP telephony. The WanderPod has a massive coverage area of 12.5 million square feet. The WanderPod is small, lightweight and easy to maneuver into small locations, a dream come true for a live event producer since connectivity is usually the biggest hurdle when encoding on-site at a live event.

Results

For starters, we've all heard some pretty crazy numbers thrown around after a webcast. Those inflated numbers can be attributed in part to applying irrelevant metrics to a live event, confusing such notions as page hits, views, requests, stream requests, successful stream requests, and simultaneous stream requests with more accurate reporting.

Reporting properly and accurately should be a webcast producer's first responsibility when delivering numbers to a client. For the two three-hour webcasts of the first and second successful launches, the events did more than 42,000 simultaneous users. This means that at any given time, 42,000 people were watching the webcasts. In comparison to other events, the average webcast on the Internet has between 1,000 to 2,000 simultaneous users. For this event, the large numbers were also partially attributed to the fact that *CNN.com*, *Space.com*, *Yahoo.com*, *WindowsMedia.com* and other websites were pointing their traffic to the live streams on xprize.org. Over the six-hour period for both webcasts, there were 130,983 unique requests for the live video.

Other relevant figures for the X PRIZE Webcasts:

- 80% of the viewers to the webcast watched for over 60 minutes.

- 60% of the viewers came from the US, 15% from Europe, 10% from Asia, and the other 15% were from other countries all over the world.

- Since the events were held during the morning in U.S. Pacific Standard Time, the majority of the live viewers were based in the U.S. and Europe. Within 24 hours of the video being available on-demand, however, there were 621,901 views, and more than 75% of those came from outside the US.

More important than the numbers is the fact that streaming media technology allowed the X PRIZE Foundation to gain mainstream exposure to their website, got people excited in what they were working to accomplish, and helped them accept donations to further their cause of bringing affordable private space travel to the public. In fact, on-line donations for the year were doubled during the two-week event thanks to exposure from the webcast.

No other type of technology could have enabled the X PRIZE foundation to broadcast this event live to the world. Considered an unqualified success, the X PRIZE foundation's use of streaming media technology has only just begun. They plan on a series of webcasts when they launch the X PRIZE CUP (*www.xpcup.com*), where the audience can come and watch the next generation of space vehicles, talk to the astronauts, and learn about space flight technology.

ACLU Members Conference

In 2004, the ACLU decided to webcast their members conference as a service to their members who were unable to attend, and also for publicity purposes. 2004 was an election year in the US, and several highly contentious issues were being tackled by the ACLU. The list of speakers and topics was impressive, and it looked set to be an impressive event.

Implementation

The A/V feeds were taken from the on-site production, which was producing the video feed that was being projected onto two large screens at either side of the stage. The production crew kindly provided separate video feeds from each camera, so the webcast crew could produce their own switched feed. One of the video feeds was noisy, so the A/V crew kindly provided a humbucker, which quickly resolved the problem

Encoding was done on-site using rented computer equipment. The rental units had to have video capture cards installed, in this case Osprey 100s. The event was being encoded in both Windows Media and Real, at broadband and dial-up rates. Six computers were rented, providing two spares for redundancy. After the cards were installed, Windows Media and Real encoding software was installed and configured.

Connectivity was provided by the hotel where the event was being held. Although the connectivity was not tested in advance, a scouting trip was taken two weeks before the event, during which extensive discussions were had with the IT and hotel events department. These discussions were invaluable later, as it established a working relationship between the webcast and hotel crews. Distribution was done via the Speedera network, which provided real-time statistics via their SpeedEye interface.

All setup and testing was done the day before the conference. Setup went relatively smoothly, though a connectivity problem was eventually detected. After extensive testing and troubleshooting, it was discovered that the switch that had been provided by the hotel was faulty. The hotel IT department was incredibly responsive, and provided replacement equipment quickly.

One member of the webcast crew taped over the plug that provided power to the webcast station with gaffer's tape. This was done because at a previous webcast someone had unwittingly unplugged the power to the entire webcasting operation. The tape would make it much harder for a mistake like this to be made.

Unfortunately, we did not do the same with our connectivity. At one point during the broadcast we lost connectivity, and turned around to see a hotel security employee staring at the phone line he had just unplugged from the wall. We screamed, he plugged it back in, and we were back online seconds later.

Though the event was webcast more or less from start to finish, the archives were edited down by topic or speaker. Editing was done on site, and the files then FTPed up to the archive streaming servers.

Results

The ACLU members conference was attended by approximately 1,000 people. Every day, approximately 500 unique viewers tuned in to the live broadcasts. While this is a relatively modest audience, it should be considered a success given the type of programming, which is only going to appeal to a relatively small number of people. Another way of looking at it is that the ACLU was able to increase attendance by 50% using webcast technology.

However, the story doesn't end there. Archive file views began as soon as they were posted. One of the archive files included footage of Seymour Hersh revealing some of his findings about abuses in the Abu Graib prison. Word got out, initially via blogs, and then via highly trafficked web sites, including MoveOn.org and MichaelMoore.com.

Within the first 30 days after the webcast, over 60,000 people had watched clips from the webcast, with most of those views being the Seymour Hersh clip. Although this incurred a substantial bandwidth charge for the ACLU, it still represented a huge success. No other mass medium could have provided the reach that the Internet provided for the same cost.

The Sweet Adelines Convention

Sweet Adelines is an international organization dedicated to female choral groups, in particular barbershop quartets. Each year they have an annual convention and competition. The 2004 convention was held in Indianapolis, and the Sweet Adelines wanted to webcast the event for all the members that would be unable to attend, as well as friends and relatives of the competitors.

Implementation

The event was held in the city convention center. Sweet Adelines have had conventions for many years (this was the 58th annual convention) and had an established in-house production team that worked with third-party vendors to provide audio and video services. The webcast team was stationed backstage with the A/V production.

Audio and video feeds were provided by the A/V production team, who were producing the feeds for the projections screens and the PA system. In a cost savings maneuver, Sweet Adelines decided that they were going to broadcast audio only feeds during the semi finals, which encompassed the first two days of the broadcast. The finals would be broadcast in video, with dial-up and broadband feeds available.

There was no scouting trip undertaken for this broadcast, as the client would not approve budget to do so. Although there was extensive communication between the convention center personnel (connectivity), the production company (A/V), and the webcasting firm, this would later come back to haunt the webcast as there simply was not enough pre-event planning. In fact, this webcast was plagued with problems.

The first problem was the encoding machines. These were rented and due to arrive two days before the event. One of the machines was misplaced by the shipping company, and did not arrive until the third day of the webcast, which left the webcast crew short one backup machine. To make matters worse, one of the machines was so badly infected with spyware that it could not be made to run at all, and it succeeded in infecting another computer nearby. This brought the number of machines in service down to four, the bare minimum needed to do the webcast.

Of course, the problems didn't stop there. This webcast was also being run through the Speedera Network, and they were experiencing odd server behavior. Their solution was to have us run redundant encodes, one to their east coast server array, the other to their west coast server array. Because we were short on backup machines, we were unable to do this, and consequently there was a 40 minute outage during the finals broadcast on the second to last day.

Finally, we were surprised when two people came by to take a look at the webcast station, and told us they'd be back for the live commentary during the finals. After a flurry of email and cell phone calls, it turned out that we were responsible for setting up and mixing a live commentary into the webcast. Not only that, but the commentators would need to be in front of the stage and in full view of the audience—100 feet away from our webcasting station.

Luckily, the production company was extremely helpful, and provided microphones and sufficient cabling to reach the live commentators. Had the production company not had spare microphones and cables, we would have been unable to meet the client's needs. Of course, they claimed that it was in their contract for the webcast. The only problem was that this information had never been relayed to the webcast crew.

Results

Given the number of problems encountered, getting this webcast off the ground turned out to be much more difficult than expected. And given the nature of the content, we didn't believe the Sweet Adelines when they told us they'd have two thousand concurrent viewers. Who wants to watch a female choral competition?

As it turns out, almost exactly two thousand people, at any given time. Sweet Adelines knew their market extremely well. The semi-finals drew audiences in the 500–1000 concurrent listeners, but the finals brought everyone back. Nearly 80,000 streams were served over the course of four days, and nearly two terabytes of data was delivered.

Sweet Adelines had an interesting approach to underwriting the cost of the webcast: voluntary donations. Access to the streams was free for everyone, but under the links to the streams was a request for donations. The suggested donation was $10. Though they wouldn't reveal exactly how many donations they received, they did say that the donations were a significant contribution to the overall cost.

Sweet Adelines consider the webcast an integral part of their annual conventions, and continue to webcast to this day. They are now offering sponsorship and advertising opportunities during the webcast. For a nominal $15 fee, the announcers will read statements during the broadcast, either congratulating competitors, or advertising products targeted to the female barbershop demographic. This is a perfect example of using the Internet to reach a niche audience that would otherwise be ignored.

Conclusion

Webcasts are undertaken nearly every day, for many different purposes, and from many different locations. Given enough time to plan and sufficient budget, you can produce a successful webcast from just about anywhere, even the middle of a desert.

Things can and eventually will go wrong during a webcast. If you've planned well, you should be able to work your way out of any situation. Don't skimp on your backups—be sure to bring plenty of extra equipment, because you never know when a client is going to ask for something they claim has been part of the webcast all along.

Finally, you don't have to have an audience of millions for a webcast to be considered a success. The idea is to satisfy a need or provide a service within the budgetary constraints. Many events already have all the production resources you'll require—all that is left is the encoding and distribution. Unlike traditional broadcasting, however, each additional viewer incurs an incremental cost, because you'll be using more bandwidth. Be sure to plan for sufficient bandwidth, and a large enough budget to pay for it.

Good luck, and welcome to the world of webcasting.

APPENDIX

Uses of Streaming and Digital Media Report

In Q1 of 2004, Aberdeen Group and *StreamingMedia.com* administered two separate surveys to visitors to the *StreamingMedia.com* website. The surveys asked respondents about their usage of streaming and digital media in a business and personal context. It also asked them about their patterns of use of rich media, including frequency, session length, and preferred media players. This appendix summarizes the survey responses and provides Aberdeen's analysis of the data. Most importantly, this appendix translates that data and analysis into specific recommendations and the direct impact for enterprises, content providers, and end-users of digital media.

We have included the Executive Summary of the report that gives the facts and figures based on the findings. More information on the entire 70-page report is available at *http://www.streamingmedia.com/research*.

Statistically Significant Research Data

Unlike many surveys conducted in the past on streaming and digital media, these surveys have a statistically significant respondent base. Thus, the results and analysis are defensible as an empirical benchmark against which readers can gauge their own use of business and personal applications and upon which future trend analysis can be conducted.

The *StreamingMedia.com* website receives more than 50,000 unique visits per month, with more then 25,500 individuals receiving its weekly newsletter, Streaming Media Xtra. The survey created by Aberdeen Group received 918 valid responses; the survey created by StreamingMedia.com received 2,043 valid responses. Those levels provide a 99% confidence level with a confidence interval of ±3%. In other words, the responses to the survey represent StreamingMedia.com's population.

The next logical question is, does the StreamingMedia.com population represent the general public, buyers of the streaming technologies, Web surfers, or other some other subgroup of the general population? The respondent overview in Chapter Two of the report presents the aggregated demographics of the respondent base. Individual readers of the entire report should use Chapter Two to determine how close the respondent base is to their target population, be that internal users, external customers, or potential buyers of technologies and services.

Aberdeen Group has performed all of the analysis and recommendations included in this report. Aberdeen analyzed the data as a total group and in several subgroups: by company size and by interest group, which is how the respondents themselves classified their "interest in streaming and digital media" per a specific survey question. The subgroup analysis is not so statistically significant as the overall data set; the confidence level for some of these subgroups drops to 95%. Chapter Two presents the response levels of the subgroups. Readers should use Chapter Two to determine the statistical significance of any specific of the subgroups in comparison with the aggregated data.

Findings Contained in the Report

This report contains statistically significant measurements of:

- Usage rates of business and personal applications that involve streaming and digital media, with segment analysis by company size and interest group, for today and for the next 12 months
- Planned spending on streaming and outsourced technologies, services, and applications for the next 12 months
- For business respondents, the percentage of company sites currently enabled for streaming or digital media
- User frequency and session length of streaming media sessions, with segment analysis by company size and interest group
- Media player installed base and user preference
- Adoption rates of file sharing, subscription, and for-pay content services

Each of the data sets is presented in table or graph format and includes Aberdeen's analysis of what is important or noteworthy. Aberdeen also highlights the relevant implications, recommendations, and impact for enterprises, content providers, and end-users.

StreamingMedia.com believes this report is the first statistically valid benchmark of the streaming and rich media market. Although the population for this study may not represent 100% of the market at large, it is highly representative of individuals, businesses, and suppliers that have an active interest in streaming and digital media.

Executive Summary
Streaming and Digital Media Are Ready for Prime Time

Aberdeen has followed the technologies and services that make up the streaming and digital media marketplace for the last four years. In Aberdeen's analysis, the market has gone from hype (1999) to hurt (2001) to helpful (2003). Over this period, some companies jumped in feet first, only to find the technologies and users were not mature enough to use the media effectively. In this report, Aberdeen proves that now is the time to aggressively engage—or re-engage—in using streaming and digital media in business and personal applications, for cost savings, revenue opportunities, and customer interaction. The reader has heard this claim before. However, the numbers are new. This statistically valid benchmark study points the way to streaming and digital media success and reveals the following findings:

- A mature, experienced user base now exists. Enterprises and content providers can now deploy streaming and digital media confident that internal employees and external customers have a solid experience with media in a variety of contexts.

- Firms that have deployed streaming applications in some business areas (e.g., distance learning, Webcasting) should look to other applications (e.g., product launches, executive communications) that build on those successes.

- Company executives, IT professionals, and content providers who are dabbling in media usage should move full-force toward expanding their deployments.

This report has real numbers to show that users are actively engaging the streaming and digital media applications available to them. The Executive Summary highlights the key findings from this report in relation to business applications and use, personal applications and use, and overall media usage.

Highlights of Business Application Usage

The following summarizes the top-level findings for business application usage from the survey results.

Business Applications with Media Approaching 50% Adoption in the Coming Year —
Most business applications with streaming or digital media components have a solid current use, with 25% to 35% of respondents regularly using rich media in company meetings, distance learning, external corporate announcements, and internal executive communications. Respondents also show a consistent projected adoption of business applications with streaming or digital media over the next 12 months, with total potential usage approaching 50% of users.

Contrary to expectations, sales force training trails most other business applications, with a little more than 20% of respondents reporting current use and only 38% indicating potential adoption of these applications in the next 12 months. Vendors regularly tout sales force training as the largest category, which is not the case. Rather, Webcasting and Web conferencing are the leading business applications for streaming and digital media.

Enterprises should compare their current use of these applications with the survey results and ask themselves, Am I a leader or laggard? Leaders in one application should examine other applications with similar adoption rates for opportunities to increase the leverage of their IT investments in digital media. Laggards can use this analysis to determine where to start: High-use applications will be less expensive and more mature than the low-use applications.

Vendors regularly tout sales force training as the largest category, which is not the case. Rather, Webcasting and Web conferencing are the leading business applications for streaming and digital media.

Spending on Media Apps in 2004 is Not Strong — Despite the economic upturn, suppliers in the streaming and digital media industry should plan on another tough year. Survey respondents said that their average spending per company for the coming year would be less than $100,000 for products and services and less than $50,000 for outsourced broadcast services. Only 5% of respondents expect to spend more than $1 million in the next 12 months.

Aberdeen research indicates that at least part of this low projected spending level is caused by the milestone approach to IT spending: buyers may plan for the overall investment, but they do not commit real dollars until specified milestones are reached. They purchase for one location or one application, get results from that segment, and then spend more only if the results are positive.

Spending per company for the coming year will be less than $100,000 for products and services and less than $50,000 for outsourced broadcast services.

Highlights of Personal Application Usage

The following summarizes the top-level findings for personal application usage from the survey results.

Media and Entertainment Dominate Personal Uses — The online versions of entertainment, news, and media content, such as news sites, movie trailers, and streaming radio, have the highest uptake, with more than 50% of respondents using these applications. Traditional "for-pay" categories, such as games and sports, have the lowest uptake, with less than 10% of respondent usage. Although only 27% of respondents indicated that they belong to subscription services, more than 60% have paid for online content.

These findings indicate that the best personal use of media applications is to augment other forms of media and entertainment. Subscriptions are a viable method to gather an audience, but should not be relied upon as the primary method for distributing content.

Highlights of Overall Media Usage

The following summarizes the top-level findings for overall media usage from the survey results.

Media Use is a Regular Occurrence Among All Users — Enterprises can expect that their users are already familiar with accessing media on their desktops. The survey shows that more than 50% of respondents use streaming or digital content at least once per day. Nearly 75% of respondents use online media at least two to three times per week, including the business user subsegment.

As a result, enterprises can be confident that the majority of their users, both employees and end-customers, are comfortable using media on their computers, in business and personal applications. This finding opens wide the door for expanding the use of network-delivered media in the enterprise, without fear that transitioning from traditional broadcast, videotape, or other forms of delivery will decrease usability.

Users are Conditioned to Use Media for Short Spurts — Despite the familiarity, most users are not ready to spend long periods of time consuming media on the desktop. The survey shows that users access media in short spurts, with nearly 65% of the respondents spending 30 minutes or less per session. Enterprises can be confident that their users are comfortable using media in business and personal applications.

The implication for businesses is not that longer content will not be watched: The survey did not ask about preferences for this topic, only about current habits. However, to conform to current usage patterns, enterprises should cut longer media into segments that are consumable in stages.

All Players are Installed, but Microsoft is Preferred — Enterprises and content providers can rest assured that users will be able to access media in almost any format. Microsoft Windows Media leads in installed media players, with nearly a 95% installed base, but only by a narrow margin: RealPlayer has an 87% installed base, and QuickTime has 83%. When it comes to which player users prefer, though, Microsoft is the clear leader. Users reported a 2-to-1 preference for Windows Media over RealPlayer or QuickTime.

Companies should continue making player and media server choices based on the business case: which technology best fits the needs of the application and provides the highest return on investment? Although users are comfortable with all players, to please the greatest number of users, companies should choose Microsoft technologies—as long as the business case does not preclude Windows Media because of cost, customizability, or other requirements.

Media Usage and Preferences

This section presents the research findings, analysis, and impact of survey responses in the following subject areas:

- Frequency of media use
- Length of media sessions
- Installed media players installed
- Preferred media player

This data is presented in three ways: all respondents, segmented by company size, and segmented by interest group (as classified by the respondents). Frequency of Streaming and Digital Media Usage The Aberdeen survey asked respondents the following question:

A1.   **How often do you use streaming media or digital media (audio or video streamed or downloaded over a network or the Internet) either for personal or business use?**

    a.   Once per month

    b.   Two to three times per month

    c.   Once per week

    d.   Two to three times per week

    e.   Once per day

    f.   More than once per day

Figure A-1 summarizes the aggregated responses to this question. **Figure A-2** segments responses by Company Size. **Figure A-3** segments respondents by Interest Group.

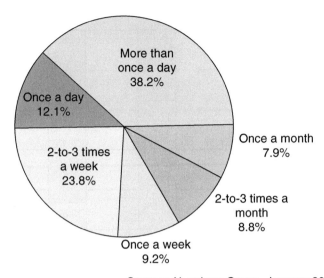

Source: Aberdeen Group, January 2004

Figure A-1

Frequency of Use—All Respondents: Most users access media at least two to three times per week.

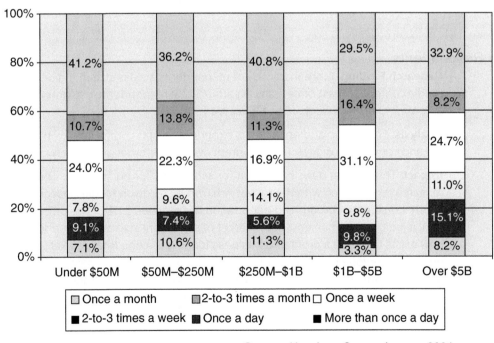

Source: Aberdeen Group, January 2004

Figure A-2

Frequency of Use—Company Size: Respondents of smaller companies are likely to use media more frequently than respondents of larger companies.

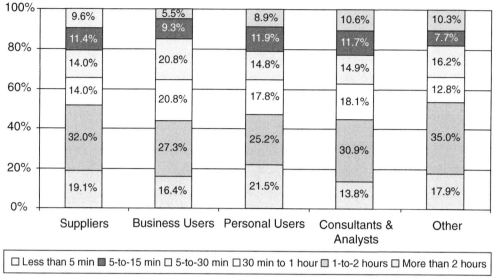

Source: Aberdeen Group, January 2004

Figure A-3
Frequency of Use—Interest Group: Most groups use streaming and digital media several times per week. Outside of the supplier community, daily use is less common.

All Respondents

- **Research Finding**: More than 50% of respondents access streaming or digital media content at least once a day. Nearly 75% of respondents use online media at least 2–3 times a week. (See **Figure A-1**.)

- **Analysis**: There is an audience that is experienced and comfortable with accessing and consuming digital media content over the Internet and IP networks.

- **Impact**: This is great news for content providers and for businesses. When this research is combined with the recent Arbitron Inc./Edison Media Research finding that residential broadband penetration has reached 21% of the U.S. population, it indicates that an end-user market of significant size and frequency of use now exists to create a profitable business for a mass consumer market—good news for everyone but content providers in particular. For businesses, the frequency indicates that users are achieving a solid experience and comfort level with streaming and digital media. That should help prevent the underlying technologies from inhibiting usage of corporate streaming media applications themselves. That is a big leap from the previous situation, where the new technologies caused more problems than they were able to solve.

Company Size

- **Research Finding**: More than half of the respondents in the small company segments said that they use media at least once per day. Respondents in less than half of the large company segments use media at least once per day. For usage of more than two to three times per week, all segments approach or exceed 75% (**Figure A-2**).

- **Analysis**: Users at companies of all sizes commonly use streaming and digital media, with a higher frequency in smaller companies.

- **Impact**: Enterprises considering expanding their streaming and digital media programs can be assured that, because of regular usage, their users are already quite comfortable with the format.

Interest Group

- **Research Finding**: Suppliers are by far the largest users of streaming and digital media, with almost 64% of supplier respondents using media at least once per day. Few personal users access media on a daily basis (more than 33%), but approach 65% at two to three times per week (**Figure A-3**).

- **Analysis**: Although company size closely reflects the aggregate data, there are significant variations when examining the data by interest group. Personal users, who are expected to be the largest user group, are actually not nearly as heavy users as suppliers. Business users, presumed to be enterprise or corporate users who are not suppliers of streaming and digital media technologies and services, have a strong base.

- **Impact**: It is no surprise that suppliers use streaming and digital media the most frequently. It is surprising, however, that the business group uses media more frequently than personal users. One implication is that businesses are requiring more use of streaming and digital media, which drives up the frequency of use. However, no correlation analysis has been performed at this time to associate business applications to business usage, although this analysis is available upon request.

Session Length of Streaming and Digital Media

The Aberdeen survey asked respondents the following question:

A2. **How long is your typical session when using streaming or digital media?**

    a.   Less than 5 minutes

    b.   5 to 15 minutes

    c.   15 to 30 minutes

    d.   30 minutes to 1 hour

    e.   1–2 hours

    f.   More than 2 hours

Figure A-4 summarizes the aggregated responses to this question. **Figure A-5** segments responses by company size. **Figure A-6** segments respondents by interest group.

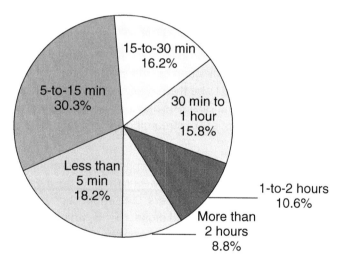

Source: Aberdeen Group, January 2004

Figure A-4
Length of Session—All: More users access shorter media segments.

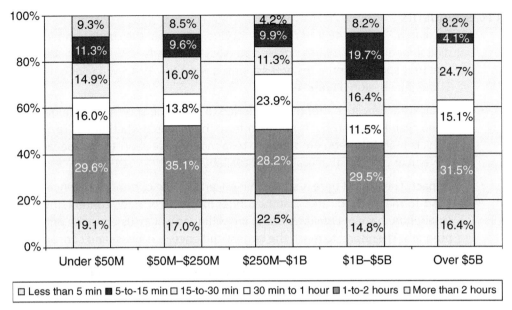

Source: Aberdeen Group, January 2004

Figure A-5

Length of Session—Company Size: Segmentation analysis of session length does not vary significantly from the aggregate data set.

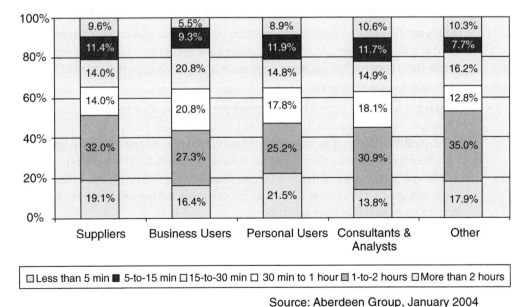

Source: Aberdeen Group, January 2004

Figure A-6

Length of Session—Interest Group: Segmentation analysis of session length does not vary significantly from the aggregate data set.

All Respondents

- **Research Finding**: 48% of respondents indicated that they use streaming or digital media for 15 minutes or less per session. Nearly 65% of respondents said that they spend 30 minutes or less per session. Only 19.4% will spend more than 1 hour per session (**Figure A-4**).

- **Analysis**: Users are currently conditioned to consume short-format audio and video over IP networks. It is not clear from the research whether this results from a chicken-and-the-egg problem: Do respondents use short-format because they prefer it or because that is all that is available?

- **Impact**: The impact here is somewhat uncertain. The current prevalence of short-format use indicates that the longer the audio or video content, the smaller the base of consumers who are willing to watch/listen to the entire program. Therefore, to reach the largest audience, business- and consumer-oriented companies should create content that is less than 15 minutes. Longer content may be able to reach the large audience if it is broken into discrete, sub-15-minute segments that can easily be stopped, restarted, and skipped. However, given that the analysis neither asked respondents how long they are willing to use digital media nor correlated availability with usage, the issue needs further research before any strong conclusions can be drawn.

Company Size and Interest Group

- **Research Finding**: In terms of session length, both company size analysis and interest group analysis echo closely the aggregate data set (**Figures A-5** and **A-6**).

- **Analysis**: The lack of significant variation by company size or interest group contains the same ambiguity as the aggregate: Is there no variation because only short-form content is available or because users prefer shorter content? This is a question for future analysis.

- **Impact**: It would be premature to advise particular actions based on this data. However, content providers, enterprises, and suppliers can infer that most users are conditioned to consume content that is less than 30 minutes in length. This conditioning should be taken into account when designing new streaming or digital media services. Anything longer than 30 minutes may necessitate behavioral changes for the general user, which can increase the challenge to market acceptance and wide user adoption.

Media Players: Installed

The Aberdeen and Streamingmedia.com surveys both asked respondents the following question:

A9/SM11: **Which of the following media players do you have installed on your desktop (check all that apply):**

    a.   Windows Media Player from Microsoft

    b.   RealPlayer from RealNetworks

    c.   QuickTime Player from Apple

    d.   MPEG player

    e.   Customized player

    f.   Other

Figure A-7 summarizes the responses to the surveys.

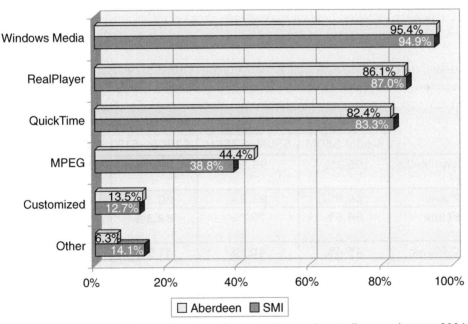

Source: Aberdeen Group and streamingmedia.com, January 2004

Figure A-7
Media Players Installed—All: Microsoft leads in installed players by a narrow margin.

All Respondents

- **Findings**: Microsoft has the highest installed penetration among respondents; nearly 95% reported that Windows Media Player is installed on their desktops. RealPlayer is close behind with an 87% installed base, and QuickTime has 83%. MPEG players are installed on nearly 39% of desktops, and customized players are installed on less than 13% of desktops (**Figure A-7**). Analysis: Most users have several media players installed.

- **Impact**: Aberdeen research shows that, behind the firewall, most companies choose one format and require their users to view content in that format. The high installed base of all three players, Microsoft, Real, and QuickTime, guarantees that choosing any one of these formats will address a broad base of users who already have the player available. Companies that want to please the largest number of current users and deliver content in the widest preferred format should offer their content in the Microsoft format.

All Respondents Finding and Analysis

Without multiple surveys conducted over several intervals, it is not possible to determine if any of the players' installed bases are growing or shrinking. This analysis will be conducted in future studies.

This research does not correlate cost of delivery with format of delivery. Companies evaluating streaming media platforms should also evaluate the licensing and maintenance costs of all available options before selecting a specific media format. See **Figure A-8**.

	Under $50M	$50M–$250M	$250M–$1B	$1B–$5B	Over $5B
Windows Media Player	95.2%	96.5%	96.0%	97.9%	97.1%
RealPlayer	86.8%	83.2%	90.3%	91.5%	83.5%
QuickTime Player	84.5%	77.7%	82.3%	84.0%	74.1%
MPEG Player	45.4%	40.1%	41.9%	51.1%	38.8%
Customized Player	13.9%	10.4%	12.1%	16.0%	12.2%
Other	6.9%	3.0%	4.0%	8.5%	5.0%

Source: streamingmedia.com, January 2004.

Figure A-8
Media players installed, by company size: Mostly mirrors aggregate data set, with variances.

- Microsoft's Windows Media Player remains the leader in all segments, with a low of 95.2% in the less than $50M segment and a high of 97.9% in the $1B–$5B segment.

- RealNetworks' RealPlayer rises slightly over the aggregated data set in two segments, reaching a 90.3% installed base in the $250M–$1B segment and a 91.5% installed base in the $1B–$5B segment. RealNetworks falls slightly in two segments, dropping to an 83.2% installed base in the $50M–$250M segment and an 83.5% installed base in the more than $5B segment.

- Apple QuickTime reflects the aggregate for three segments (less than $50M: 84.5%; $250M–$1B: 82.3%; and $1B–$5B: 84.0%). Apple falls in the other segments, to 77.7% in the $50M–$250M segment and to 74.1% in the more than $5B segment.

- The MPEG player reflects the aggregate dataset except for a significant jump in the "$1B–$5B" segment, reaching 51.1%.

- The customized player and other categories see no significant difference from the aggregate data set. Impact: Enterprises should work with application developers to determine the most appropriate platform for their internal content and applications.

Company Size Finding and Analysis

- Microsoft's Windows Media Player remains the leader in all interest group segments and does not vary significantly from the aggregate results (from 94.9% to 96.6%). See **Figure A-9.**

	Suppliers	Business	Personal	Consultants	Other
Windows Media Player	96.6%	94.9%	96.0%	96.3%	91.8%
RealPlayer	87.7%	86.1%	81.6%	83.5%	86.0%
QuickTime Player	84.4%	82.1%	81.6%	79.4%	79.8%
MPEG Player	46.7%	44.6%	37.6%	44.5%	39.5%
Customized Player	16.2%	11.2%	7.2%	12.8%	14.4%
Other	7.7%	5.3%	8.0%	4.1%	5.3%

Source: streamingmedia.com, January 2004.

Figure A-9
Media players installed, by interest group: Mostly mirrors aggregate data set, with variances.

- RealNetworks' RealOne Player remains steady for the supplier and business user segments (87.7% and 86.1%, respectively), but drops to 83.5% in the consultant/analyst segment and to 81.6% in the personal user segment.

- Apple QuickTime is steady, with a high of 84.4% in the supplier segment and a low of 79.4% in the consultant/analyst segment.

- The MPEG player is also steady, with a low of 37.6% of the personal users and a high of 47.6% among suppliers.

- The customized player and other categories see no significant difference from the aggregate data set.

Impact: The drop against the aggregated data set in installed base of RealPlayer and Quick-Time in the personal segment indicates that, if enterprises or content providers want to reach the widest possible audience, they should use the Microsoft platform. Again, further research is required to determine the growth pattern of any of these installed base segments.

Additional analysis and impact studies of the installed base of media players are available upon request from Aberdeen.

Media Players: Preferred

The Aberdeen survey asked respondents the following question:

A10.　**If given a choice, which format do you prefer to use　(check ONLY ONE):**

    a.　MPEG player

    b.　QuickTime (Apple)

    c.　RealMedia (RealNetworks)

    d.　Windows Media (Microsoft)

    e.　Other

Figure A-10 summarizes the aggregated responses to the survey.

All Respondents

- **Findings**: Microsoft was selected as the preferred player by 40% of respondents. RealPlayer edged out QuickTime for second place, as these players finished with 22% and 21%, respectively. MPEG players garnered only 12% of player preference (**Figure A-10**).

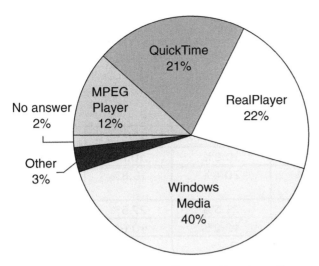

Source: Aberdeen Group, January 2004

Figure A-10
Media Player Preferred, All: Microsoft has a significant lead. QuickTime and RealPlayer are practically equal.

- **Analysis**: Microsoft is clearly the player of choice and has the highest penetration rate. The near-even split between RealPlayer and QuickTime is interesting but only a starting point for further research: Tracking this question over time will provide better insight into whether Apple will overtake RealNetworks, or if format preferences have reached stabilization.

- **Impact**: When combined with the installed base results, this question reinforces the recommendation that enterprises and content providers that seek to reach the widest possible audience should use Windows Media format. RealPlayer and QuickTime are also important options, particularly for content providers trying to please the majority of the potential user base.

Company Size Findings and Analysis

- Microsoft's Windows Media Player remains the preferred player in all segments. There is a significant jump over the aggregate data set in the $1B–$5B subsegment, with a preference of 49.2%, and less significant but still relevant bump in the $50M–$250M segment, to 45.2%. Refer to **Figure A-11**.

	Under $50M	$50M–$250M	$250M–$1B	$1B–$5B	Over $5B
MPEG Player	12.2%	10.8%	10.1%	9.8%	13.7%
QuickTime Player	23.9%	20.4%	18.8%	14.8%	17.8%
RealPlayer	21.2%	21.5%	27.5%	23.0%	19.2%
Windows Media	39.3%	45.2%	40.6%	49.2%	43.8%
Other	3.3%	2.2%	2.9%	3.3%	5.5%

Source: Aberdeen Group, January 2004.

Figure A-11
Media players preferred, company size. Mostly minor aggregate data set, with variances.

- Preference for RealPlayer reflects the aggregate data, with the exception of the $250M–$1B segment, where preference rises to 27.5%.

- Preference for QuickTime remains steady in most company segments, but drops to 14.8% in the largest segment.

- There is no significant difference based on company size in preference for MPEG player over the aggregated data set.

Impact: The sharp increase in preference for Microsoft in the top segment is significant, indicating that Microsoft has a controlling critical mass in this segment. Further study is required to determine the source of the jump and whether the difference will hold with a broader data set than the streamingmedia.com respondents.

Interest Group Data Set Findings

- Windows Media and RealPlayer preferences by interest group do not vary significantly from the aggregated data set. Refer to **Figure A-12**.

	Suppliers	Business	Personal	Consultants	Other
MPEG Player	14.0%	11.5%	8.2%	16.3%	4.5%
QuickTime Player	20.5%	17.6%	26.1%	22.8%	23.6%
RealPlayer	20.5%	23.6%	23.9%	18.5%	29.1%
Windows Media	41.8%	43.4%	38.1%	39.1%	39.1%
Other	3.1%	3.8%	3.7%	3.3%	3.6%

Source: Aberdeen Group, January 2004.

Figure A-12
Media players preferred, by interest group: significant variations from the aggregate.

- Preference for QuickTime tracks the aggregate data set, except among personal users, where preference jumps to 26.1%. The shift is at the expense of MPEG players, which falls to 8.2%.

Analysis: The shift in the personal user subsegment from MPEG to QuickTime is not so significant as the numbers may indicate. Because QuickTime is built from the MPEG code base and the informed nature of the respondent base (see Chapter Two), respondents are likely to see both QuickTime and MPEG as two flavors of the same technology. This analysis also reflects other research that indicates that informed user groups see MPEG and QuickTime players as somewhat interchangeable.

Impact: The consistency of results for Microsoft and Real between the aggregate set and the interest group segments indicates that users have the same preferences, regardless of the type of user they are.

Glossary

Artifact: Something in an audio or video file that wasn't there in the first place. Artifacts are introduced by audio and video streaming codecs, or by the conversion process between video or audio formats.

Aspect Ratio: The ratio of the width to the height of a video frame. Standard definition video uses a 4:3 aspect ratio. Widescreen video uses a 16:9 aspect ratio.

BOC (Broadcast Operations Center): Where webcast distribution takes place. If raw audio and video feeds are sent back to the BOC, encoding can take place here.

Broadband: Any non-dial-up Internet connection, generally assumed to be above 200 kbps.

Cache: An area used to temporarily store information. On a computer this can be in high-speed RAM memory as opposed to a hard-drive. On the Internet, files may be *cached* on a local server as opposed to a server farther away.

Chrominance: The color component of a video signal

Codec: Software that determines how to encode and decode streaming media files. Streaming media codecs use perceptual models to determine how to retain as much fidelity as possible.

Compression (audio): An audio signal processing technique whereby portions of audio programming that exceed a certain threshold are attenuated. Compression is often used to protect input levels from distortion caused by sudden peaks in the audio programming. It is also used to even out the overall levels throughout a program.

Compression (file size): A technique used to reduce the size of digitized files. Many common Internet file types such as JPEG, GIF, and PNG utilize compression to achieve their reduced file sizes. They use what is known as "lossy" compression, where the resulting file is only an approximation of the original. In loss-less compression, such as .zip files, the original file(s) can be recreated exactly.

Constant Bit Rate (CBR): An approach to encoding data that keeps the bit rate constant throughout. This approach is more suited to streaming media.

Decibel (dB): A unit of measure used in audio that measures the power of an audio signal. It is a logarithmic measure so each increase of 3 dB means a doubling of power. To complicate matters, there are various types of decibels: dBU, dBV, and so on. In this book we use the term in its most generic form.

Deinterlacing: A process that attempts to remove the artifacts from an interlaced signal. (see *Interlacing*)

Difference frame: In a compressed video sequence, a frame that contains only the information about the current frame that is different from the previous frame. Difference frames require key frames as a reference.

DNS (Dynamic Name Service or System): The system by which Internet server names, such as www.streamingmedia.com are translated into IP addresses, such as 192.68.1.100.

DRM (Digital Rights Management): Digital rights management schemes are used to protect content from unlawful use. For instance, some DRM schemes prevent you from swapping music with other people online, or from burning CDs.

Equalization (EQ): An audio signal processing technique that changes harmonic or tonal character by boosting or attenuating certain frequency ranges in an audio signal. Desired frequencies can be turned up, or boosted, while undesired frequencies or noise can be turned down, or attenuated. An everyday example would be the bass and treble adjustments on your home stereo.

Field: One-half of an interlaced video frame, consisting of either the odd or the even numbered scan lines.

Firewall: A security system designed to allow only certain kinds of traffic in and out of networks. They can be implemented in hardware or software, and can block data packets based on a number of different security criteria, such as port number or protocol type. Firewalls often block streaming media traffic because it uses non-standard port numbers.

FireWire: See *IEEE 1394*.

Gain: In audio terms, gain refers to the amount of amplification being applied. Similarly, the gain structure of an audio setup refers to the amount of amplification being applied at each stage.

Gating (noise gate): A form of audio signal processing where everything below a set threshold is muted. It can be useful as a noise reduction technique.

Headroom (audio): The difference between the maximum signal a system can reproduce without distortion and the standard operating level.

Hertz (Hz): A unit of measure, generally used for audio frequency. One cycle per second is equal to one Hertz (Hz). The human hearing range extends from 20–20,000 Hz, or 20-20 kHz. In this case, the "k" stands for 1000 instead of 1024 as is generally assumed in computer applications.

Hotspot: A particular area or segment of a clip that links to another clip or presentation. Hotspots can be defined spatially and temporally.

IEEE: Pronounced "I-triple-E", the Institute of Electrical and Electronics Engineers, Inc. An organization dedicated to promoting standards in computing and electrical engineering.

IEEE 1394 (also known as FireWire or iLink): An IEEE standard for exchanging digital information at rates of 100, 200, or 400 megabits per second. Originally developed by Apple and trademarked as FireWire, it was standardized by the IEEE 1394 working group. iLink is Sony's implementation of the IEEE 1394 standard.

iLink: See *IEEE 1394*.

Interlacing: The system used by television displays and cameras whereby each frame is divided into odd lines and even lines. Each group of odd and even lines is referred to as a *field*. The combination of the two fields, displayed in rapid succession, makes up one frame of video. (see *Field; Deinterlacing*)

Inverse Telecine: The process of removing the extra fields in a video signal that result from the Telecine process. Removing these redundant fields leads to greater encoding efficiency.

ISP (Internet Service Provider): A company that provides access to the Internet, often also offering server hosting, stream hosting, etc.

Key Frame: In a compressed video sequence, a frame that contains information about the whole frame, as opposed to a difference frame (see *Difference frame*).

Load Balancing: A technique of distributing server requests amongst a number of servers, for redundancy and efficiency purposes. Load balancers can be software programs or hardware devices.

Luminance: The brightness portion of a video signal.

Metadata: A neologism from the Greek meta (among, with) and data, metadata is information about data. For instance, the title, author, and copyright of a presentation are metadata associated with a presentation.

Metafile: Similar to metadata, a metafile is a file that contains information about another file. Typically the metafile contains a "pointer" to the location of the file, such as a URL or a relative path.

MIDI (Musical Instrument Digital Interface): A standard used to exchange musical information between devices. Using MIDI, music sequencing software can control the playback of keyboards, samplers, or any other MIDI-compliant devices. MIDI data includes what notes to play, when to play them, how long to play them, how loud, what instrument to use, etc. MIDI data can be streamed by the RealSystem utilizing the Crescendo Forte plug-in.

MIME type: MIME (Multipurpose Internet Mail Extensions) types are used as a standard way of exchanging data over the Internet. An application can determine if it has appropriate rendering software to decode a file by looking at the MIME type. If it does not, it can hand off the file to a separate program (or plug-in). When you install new software, it generally "registers" itself for a number of different MIME types—sometimes conflicting with other applications.

Mount Point: A virtual directory on a RealServer. Mount points are used to organize streams into different types, such as live streams, streams that contain advertising, QuickTime streams, etc. (see *Publishing Point*).

Multicasting: A method of broadcasting on the Internet where all audience members share a single stream. Multicast streams are sent using the Multicast Address Space (224.0.0.0 through 239.255.255.255). Multicast packets are forwarded indiscriminately across the Internet instead of forwarded to a particular user. All multicast audience members receive copies of the data packets from their local routers. All routers involved in a multicast must be "multicast-enabled."

Namespace: An XML namespace is a collection of names used in an XML document as element types and attribute names. They consist of a prefix, which is used to refer to the namespace throughout the rest of the document, and a unique identifier that identifies the namespace. For example, in this namespace declaration of a SMIL document:

```
<smil xmlns:cv="http://features.real.com/systemComponent">
```

The prefix is cv, which can be used in the SMIL document to refer to the namespace. The namespace is *http://features.real.com/systemComponent*. Note that even though this namespace is a fully qualified URL, it is never accessed by the SMIL player and it is used only as a unique identifier.

NIC (Network Interface Card): A computer card that enables communication across a local area network.

NOC (Network Operations Center): See *BOC*.

Normalization: An audio signal processing technique that analyzes a file to discover exactly how much the volume can be turned up before distortion, and then applies that volume change. Some normalization routines allow the user to specify the level to "normalize" to as a percentage of maximum allowable volume.

NTSC (National Television Standards Committee): The broadcast standard for television signals in the United States and most of Central and South America, which specifies 30 interlaced frames per second. Each frame consists of 525 horizontal lines of resolution.

NTSC 3/2 Pulldown: Because of the differing frame rates (24 for film, 30 for NTSC) extra frames must be created. By scanning every other frame three times instead of twice, five fields are created from every two frames, yielding 60 fields total from 24 frames. The reverse process is known as Inverse Telecine (see *Inverse Telecine*). See Chapter 2 for a more detailed discussion.

OpenDML: Also known as AVI 2.0, a standard that extends the AVI specification and effectively removes the 2 Gigabyte file size limit by allowing data to be written across multiple files.

Overscan: The area of a broadcast video image that is normally hidden by the plastic surrounds of a television monitor. Sometimes this area can contain video noise and should be removed before encoding.

PAL (Phase Alternation by Line): The broadcast standard for television signals in most European countries, which specifies 25 interlaced frames per second. Each frame consists of 625 horizontal lines of resolution. PAL color is considered to be superior to NTSC.

Port (port numbers): Networking applications use ports to determine which application receives the data being sent. For instance, web browsers request data on port 80, which is assigned to HTTP traffic. When the request arrives at the destination server, it is handed to the web server. In this manner many different servers can run on the same machine, each on a different port.

Proc amp: Short for *video processing amplifier*. A proc amp is used to adjust the quality of a video signal by manipulating the brightness, contrast, and color content.

Progressive Download: A delivery technology where media files are played back as they are being downloaded. Playback cannot begin until a sufficient amount of the file has been downloaded and buffered so that playback is uninterrupted. The amount of time before playback begins is determined by the viewer's bandwidth and the size of the file.

Protocol: A standardized method of exchanging digital information, such as HTTP (Hyper-Text Transfer Protocol) or RTSP (Real Time Streaming Protocol). Different protocols use different amounts and types of error correction, compression, encryption, etc.

Publishing Point: A virtual directory on a Windows Media Server. Publishing points are used to organize streams into different types, such as live streams, multicast streams, etc. (see *Mount Point*).

Q (in relation to audio equalization): The width of the frequency band to be affected by a parametric EQ operation. Q relates to the number of octaves—a Q of 1 means one octave, centered on the chosen frequency that will be affected.

Render: A generic term meaning to convert from digital information to audio or visual display. In video editing systems, the act of committing desired special effects or transitions to the hard drive. Some effects may not be visible until the section is rendered.

SDP (Session Description Protocol) file: The file used to connect QuickTime players to live QuickTime streams. These files are created by the broadcast application and must be placed on the QuickTime streaming server in the configured media directory.

SMIL (Synchronized Multimedia Integration Language): An open, standardized language for combining multiple data types into a single multimedia presentation. SMIL is covered in detail in Part VII of this book.

Telecine: The process of transferring film content to video. (see *NTSC 3/2 Pulldown*).

Unicast: A method of Internet broadcasting whereby each audience member is sent an individual copy of a broadcast, as opposed to multicast, where a single broadcast stream is shared by all audience members (see Multicast).

Unicode: A standardized system that assigns a unique numerical value to every letters and character used in every language. There are over 94,000 Unicode characters defined, with more being added every day.

URL (Uniform Resource Locator): The URL specifies the location of a file and what protocol to use to retrieve it.

Variable Bit Rate (VBR): Variable bit rate files vary the bit rate of an encoded file so that more bits are used to encode complex video passages. In general VBR files are not suitable for streaming unless the degree of variation is limited.

Resources

Along with the webcasting information in this book, we also want to provide you with a comprehensive list of publications, websites and newsletters that can provide you with additional business and technical resources on webcasting and streaming media technology.

Websites

StreamingMedia.com
Streaming Media is the #1 online destination for professionals seeking industry news, information, articles, directories and services. The site features thousands of original articles, hundreds of hours of audio/video content, weekly newsletters read by over 100,000 subscribers and a wide range of services and resources dedicated to the streaming media industry.

www.streamingmedia.com

DigitalWebcast.com
Digital Media Online's home page serves as a hub where digital media professionals can find the tools and information they need to get their jobs done.

www.digitalwebcast.com

Singingfish
Singingfish offers audio/video search services that help people easily find mp3s, movie trailers, sports highlights, newscasts, and other streaming files.

www.singingfish.com

Newsletters

Streaming Media Xtra

Read all about it—You can't afford to be without this weekly e-Newsletter—sign up today to get your breaking Streaming Media news.

www.streamingmedia.com/subscribe.asp

Stream This!

Developed exclusively for "industry" executives, the Dan Rayburn "Stream This!" monthly newsletter is the best Compilation of News & Information For Streaming Media "Insiders

www.danrayburn.com

DigitalMediaWire

Considered a "must read" by industry insiders, the DigitalMediaWire newsletter delivers concise and timely briefings on key business, legal & finance issues impacting digital media each business day.

www.digitalmediawire.com

DigitalMusicNews

Receive the Digital Music News Daily Email.

www.digitalmusicnews.com

Google

Google News Alerts are sent by email when news articles appear online that match the topics you specify.

www.google.com/newsalerts

Internet Acceleration

A Compilation of News & Events in the Internet Infrastructure Arena

www.internetacceleration.com

Circuits from NYTimes.com

Free weekly Circuits newsletter with exclusive commentary by David Pogue, the State of the Art columnist.

www.nytimes.com/pages/technology/circuits/index.html

EContent Xtra

Straight from EContent Magazine's newsdesk, the EContent Xtra email newsfeed keeps you informed of events and trends driving the content industry.

www.econtentmag.com/newsletters

Publications

Streaming Media Industry Sourcebook
The Streaming Media Industry Sourcebook is the definitive guide for implementing digital media technology and applications

www.streamingmedia.com/sourcebook

EContent Magazine
EContent magazine identifies and explains emerging digital content trends, strategies, and resources to help professionals navigate the content maze and find a clear path to profits and improved business processes.

www.econtentmag.com

Index

Printed and bound by CPI Group (UK) Ltd, Croydon, CR0 4YY

21/10/2024

01777053-0002